Italian Plaster
Techniques

Italian Plaster Techniques

Maureen Soens

Sterling Publishing Co., Inc.

New York

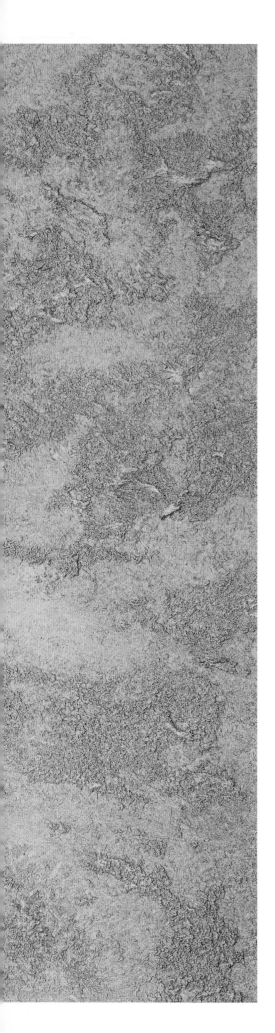

PROLIFIC IMPRESSIONS PRODUCTION STAFF:

Editor in Chief: Mickey Baskett
Copy Editor: Phyllis Mueller
Graphics: Dianne Miller, Karen Turpin
Styling: Lenos Key
Photography: Salter Photography, Jerry Mucklow
Administration: Jim Baskett

Library of Congress Cataloging-in-Publication Data
Soens, Maureen.
  Italian plaster techniques / Maureen Soens.
      p. cm.
  Includes index.
  ISBN 1-4027-1471-8
  1. House painting—Amateurs' manuals. 2. Interior decoration—Amateurs' manuals. 3. Texture painting—Amateurs' manuals. 4. Plastering—Amateurs' manuals. 5. Interior walls—Decoration—Amateurs' manuals. I. Title.

TT323.S64 2005
698—dc22

2004028541

10 9 8 7 6 5 4 3 2 1

Published by Sterling Publishing Co., Inc.
387 Park Avenue South, New York, N.Y. 10016

© 2005 by Prolific Impressions, Inc.
Produced by Prolific Impressions, Inc.
160 South Candler St., Decatur, GA 30030

Distributed in Canada by Sterling Publishing
c/o Canadian Manda Group, 165 Dufferin Street
Toronto, Ontario, Canada M6K 3H6
Distributed in Great Britain by Chrysalis Books Group PLC,
The Chrysalis Building, Bramley Road, London W10 6SP, England
Distributed in Australia by Capricorn Link (Australia) Pty. Ltd.
P.O. Box 704, Windsor, NSW 2756 Australia

Printed in China

For information about custom editions, special sales, premium and corporate purchases, please contact Sterling Special Sales Department at 800-805-5489 or specialsales@sterlingpub.com.

Sterling ISBN 1-4027-1471-8

About the Artist
MAUREEN SOENS

While her children were growing up, Maureen Soens' enthusiasm for the decorative arts evolved into a new career in decorative painting that eventually included stenciling, faux finishes, wood graining, murals, and plaster finishes for residences and businesses. Her work can be seen in homes, churches, restaurants, medical facilities, and offices in the United States and in Naworth Castle, Brampton, Cumbria, England.

Maureen became a Certified Instructor for Adele Bishop, Inc. in 1983. She joined the Stencil Artisans League in 1986 and is also a member of the Stencilers and Decorative Artists Guild. She has taught classes in her home studio, in community education programs, and at national conventions. In 1996, Maureen began painting with Lynne German, a well-known artisan in the Detroit, Michigan area. Together they have led a group of decorative painters in continuing projects at Naworth Castle in England and have developed a three-day Professional Series Paint Seminar for Sherwin-Williams, Inc.

Maureen's work has been published in magazines and books and has been featured on television in Michigan and on Cumbria TV in England. She and her husband Ken live in Rochester Hills, Michigan. They are the parents of two grown children, Nicholas and Kristen.

DEDICATION

This book is dedicated to the memory of my parents, John and Mary McWilliams, who inspired me to work hard, rejoice in the new day, and give thanks.

A special thanks to the following homeowners for allowing us to photograph their homes:

Bortz	*Pokorski*	*Schwartz*
Darrish	*Purdy*	*Seid*
Dykstra	*Qonja*	*Theissen*
Markowicz	*Scarlatelli*	*Zebari*

ACKNOWLEDGMENTS

This book would not have been possible without the contributions and support of many others. My sincere thanks and appreciation to all who not only gave me the opportunity to work in their homes and businesses, but extended their hospitality by graciously allowing their rooms to be photographed. Thank you to Lynne German and Melanie Rzepecki for tirelessly working with me side by side. A special note of thanks to my friend and mentor, Jane Gauss, who was my first instructor and continues to give me the encouragement and confidence to develop my love for the arts and grow a successful business. Finally, my heartfelt love and appreciation to my husband and children for their years of acceptance – thank you, Ken, Nicholas, and Kristen for affording me the opportunity to be a wife, a mom, and a decorative painter. And thank you, Ken, for cooking those late night dinners.

Learn to Create Elegant Textured Finishes

YOU ARE ABOUT TO EMBARK ON A TRULY EXCITING HOME decorating experience! Texture on walls, furniture, floors, and accessories is the craze in home décor and crafting today. In this book, Maureen Soens brings many years of "boot-strap" learning, combined with her natural teaching ability to take you step-by-step through each texture and faux technique. The instructions are concise, and the photography will inspire you to create your own magic with texture.

Italian Plaster Techniques is so much more than a pretty picture book. Likewise, it is not a book you will initially read from cover to cover. First, you'll glance through the pages and envision these techniques in your own home. Then the step-by-step instructions will teach you how to create the finishes on your own, while allowing and encouraging your own creativity to blossom. This how-to manual will become a trusted reference for years to come.

Maureen Soens is highly respected in the professional decorative painting industry; now she shares many tips and techniques that beginners and professionals alike will find useful. I have had the privilege of working with her for more than 30 years, and I truly admire her talents and creativity. She is a gifted teacher who graciously shares herself with everyone who reads this book!

Enjoy every minute of your new decorating adventures with plaster and faux finishes, and be sure to share *Italian Plaster Techniques* with your friends.

Jane Gauss

An Ancient Art

PLASTER HAS BEEN A POPULAR means of decorating walls for centuries, and texture is enjoying a welcome revival as a way to add interest, variation, and individuality to surfaces, from old world looks that mimic stucco and marble to contemporary iridescent finishes. In the home, plaster can add a sophisticated design element.

Plaster medium is one of the oldest ideas in

surface decoration, dating back to ancient Greece. The early form of this finish was rendered from a carefully crafted mixture of natural materials such as lime, marble dust, and egg or milk solids. Artisans of the ancient principality of Venice, where the technique originated, guarded their recipes with great secrecy. Examples of Venetian plaster still exist in the rediscovered ruins of Pompeii.

Many of the recipes died with their creators, but a few survived and are used today by plaster craftsmen who continue the old world tradition. These natural formulas have a limited shelf life and don't perform consistently when mixed in large quantities.

To recreate these beautiful finishes, modern materials and techniques have been developed that allow today's crafters to replicate the rich finishes that once adorned the walls of the wealthy. Today, plaster techniques are part of the trend to include handcrafted and handpainted elements in residential and commercial environments – primitive designs as well as ornate and sophisticated ones that borrow from the past and cross the continents. In this book, I address plaster and its use on walls, furniture, and accessories.

Modern products make the plastering process much easier for do-it-yourselfers – you don't have to attend an expensive decorative painting school to learn how to use texture on walls, and you don't need high-priced products.

In this book, I've included techniques I have used for creating plaster surfaces and tips from my experience. My goal is to provide a concise manual that is user friendly for beginners and allows anyone to achieve wonderful results with the satisfaction of having done it yourself! Clear, concise instructions and numerous photographs show plaster's many applications and introduce a variety of different finishes. The possibilities are as endless as your imagination.

TYPES OF PLASTER IN THIS BOOK

This book discusses two types of plaster finishes. They can be applied tinted or untinted over drywall or plaster that has been painted.

Polished plasters, *sometimes referred to as Venetian plaster, provide visual smooth texture with a burnished or polished finish. A topcoat can be applied to seal and provide sheen. Polished plasters can also be waxed.*

Textured plasters, *which can be smooth or coarse, are sometimes referred to as textured or sculptured stone. Smooth textured plasters are products that provide*

visual and actual texture. They can be manipulated to be dimensionally raised to the touch, but resemble smooth stone.

Coarse textured plasters have a gritty quality, and the product may be slightly thicker. They can be used to create a rougher stone-like texture on walls. Coarse textured plasters are usually more opaque.

Plasters of the Old World

Polished Plaster

POLISHED PLASTER IS THE GENERIC term for **Venetian plaster.** For our purposes, the terms are interchangeable. Polished plaster is now embraced by the interior design industry in the United States in residential applications and for commercial applications such as hotel and theater lobbies.

Polished plasters are products that provide visual texture but are smooth and sleek to the touch. Thin layers of tinted plaster are applied to a surface to create visual dimension and texture.

To many observers the finish appears to be polished marble.

When the product has dried, applying pressure with the applicator blade in a circular movement over the surface – a process called burnishing – brings up the profile. (It's similar to polishing a rock.) Burnishing can be labor-intensive; sanding is an alternative to burnishing that provides sheen, as will applying a glossy acrylic topcoat or rubbing with beeswax.

POLISHED PLASTER HAS THE FOLLOWING CHARACTERISTICS:

- *Dries to a very hard, durable finish.*

- *Can be tinted with artist acrylics, universal tints*

- *Washable after a full cure when used with translucent topcoat*

- *Can be burnished to a high sheen*

- *Will take metallic, iridescent and pearlescent pigments in the clear topcoat only*

- *Can be applied over previously painted surfaces, plaster, wood, metal, plastic, etc.*

- *Quick drying -many layers can be applied on the same day.*

Textured Plasters

TEXTURED PLASTER CAN MIMIC simple, traditional stucco or carved stone or be used to create faux tile and embossed patterns. It can be applied with a blade or rolled on surfaces with a paint roller, and the finished result has a texture you can feel.

Among the techniques you'll see in this book are crosshatch, breakthrough plaster, combed plaster, stippled plaster, embossed (stamped) plaster, raised designs in plaster, Venetian lace, and faux tiles. All can be applied tinted or untinted and glazed afterward. They can be rendered in smooth or coarse textured plaster.

Textured plaster and sculptured stone are not burnished or polished. Glazing the plaster after it dries gives textured plaster more dimension.

Although the textured plaster can be tinted and applied, the added step of glazing after the plaster is dry gives the wall texture much more dimension. Glaze can be applied to both tinted and untinted plaster walls.

TEXTURED PLASTER HAS THE FOLLOWING CHARACTERISTICS:

- *A variety of textures can be created with tools, stencils, or stamps.*

- *Can be tinted with artists acrylics, universal tints or dry pigments*

- *Can be glazed with water based glazes and urethanes*

- *Can be glazed with metallic, iridescent and pearlescent glazes*

- *Can be applied over previously painted surfaces*

- *Quick drying*

The Following Textured Plaster Techniques are Included:

Crosshatch

Breakthrough Plaster

Combed Plaster

Stippled Plaster

Embossed Plaster

Raised Designs in Plaster

Venetian Lace

Faux Tiles

Plaster

The types of plaster you need for the techniques in this book are available at do-it-yourself and paint stores, some craft stores, and from online and mail order outlets. Formulated especially to mimic old world plastering techniques, the plaster has a paste-like consistency and is usually sold in one-gallon, and quart cans. There are a variety of brands on the market; they all perform in much the same way. The label on the can tells how many square feet the plaster will cover.

Plaster **for the polished plaster technique** may be labeled "Venetian plaster," "Italian plaster," or "polished plaster." It is sold both tinted and untinted. Most untinted base plasters are white; some are clear. When tinting plaster to a deep color, a clear base plaster is recommended. Clear base plasters are most readily available from online and mail order outlets.

Some stores will tint the plaster for you – you pick a

CAUTION

Plaster compounds are quick drying. To keep the plaster in the can moist while you work, keep the can covered with the lid or drape a damp towel over the open can.

---

color from their chart and they add and mix the tints, just like choosing a paint color. If you're trying to match a specific color that's not one of the choices the store offers or if you purchase plaster from a store that does not provide tinting, you will need to use universal tints to color it.

For the textured plaster techniques, you'll need plaster labeled "textured plaster" or "sculptured stone." This type of plaster is usually – but not always – sold untinted and can be labeled "smooth" or "coarse." Textured plasters that are labeled *smooth* provide actual texture. This plaster can be manipulated to be dimensionally raised to the touch, or resembles the surface of a smooth stone.

Textured plasters that are labeled *coarse* are products that have a gritty quality, and the viscosity of the product may be slightly thicker. Coarse-textured plaster can be used to create a rougher stone-like feel on your walls. It usually is a little more opaque.

TINTED OR UNTINTED?

Plasters and glazes are available untinted and tinted. Because the availability of tinted products is more limited, formulas are provided for tinting plaster and glazes for the projects in this book.

Pictured above, clockwise from top left: Tinted polished plaster, smooth textured plaster, untinted polished plaster, tinted polished plaster.

Colorants for Tinting Plaster

Universal Tints

Universal tints are liquid pigments that can be added to plaster, paint, or glaze. They are available at paint stores and in the paint departments of home improvement and hardware stores. You can mix them according to a given formula or add them, a few drops at a time, until the desired color is achieved. Always mix thoroughly for a consistent appearance.

Mica Powders

Mica powders are iridescent powders made from finely ground minerals that may be purchased at paint or art stores. They can be added to plaster or glazing medium to add color and shimmer. Be sure they are uniformly mixed with the plaster before application to ensure a consistent appearance.

TIP

IF you tint the plaster yourself, keep precise notes about the colorants you use. That way, if you run out before your project is finished and need more, you can duplicate the color.

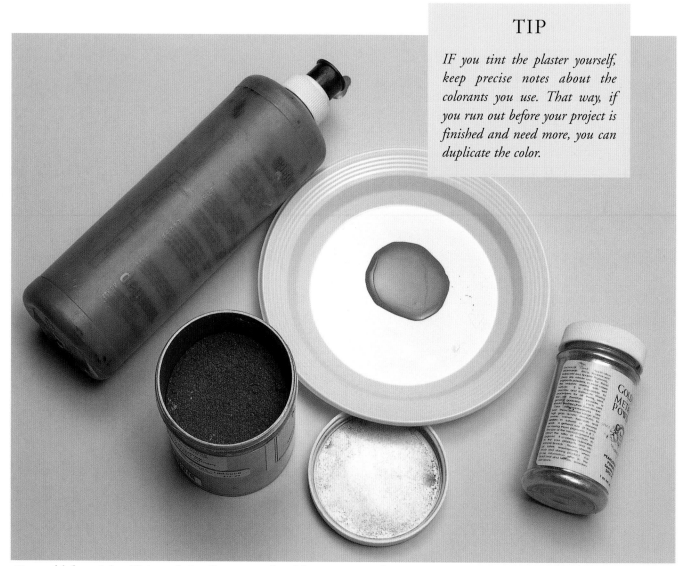

Pictured left to right: Universal tint (in squeeze bottle), two types of mica powders in jars.

Glazes & Tints for Glazes

GLAZING MEDIUM & TINTED GLAZES

Clear glazing medium is a transparent gel or liquid that comes in tubs, bottles, and cans. Waterbased glazing medium is recommended. It can be tinted with acrylic paint or universal tints and rubbed over plaster to create layers of color, highlights and texture.

There are also pre-tinted glazes available. Using a pre-tinted glaze is convenient if you can find the color and intensity you want. TIP: If you tint the glaze yourself, keep precise notes about the colorants you use. That way, if you run out before your project is finished and need more, you can duplicate the color. (One advantage of using pre-tinted glaze is that you can buy more.)

DRY PIGMENTS

Dry powder pigments can be mixed with water and rubbed over dried plaster. Find them at art supply centers. They must be sealed with a waterbased urethane topcoat.

ACRYLIC PAINT

Acrylic craft paints, which come in small squeeze bottles, can be used to tint polished plaster or glazing medium. These paints will produce less transparent results than universal tints or dry powder pigments. Find them at crafts and art supply stores.

Latex house paint can be substituted for a glaze and applied over untinted plaster for an opaque textured finish.

Pictured clockwise from top left: Clear glazing medium in a plastic tub, clear glazing medium in a plastic container, tinted glaze, acrylic craft paint, dry pigment, clear glazing medium in a can.

Tools For Applying Plaster

BLADES

You can use either metal or plastic blades – flat ones with beveled edges – for applying plaster, but metal ones are more durable. They are available in various widths, from 1" to 6". I usually work with a 4" blade on the main part of the wall and use smaller blades for tight places.

To work with plaster, use two blades that are the same size – one blade is used to scoop the plaster from the container and acts as a palette. This is called the "loading blade." The other blade is used to apply the plaster to the surface, referred to as the "action" blade.

Prepare metal blades by sanding the sharp corners with 100 grit (fine) sandpaper to round them. Wipe the blade thoroughly to remove any sanding residue.

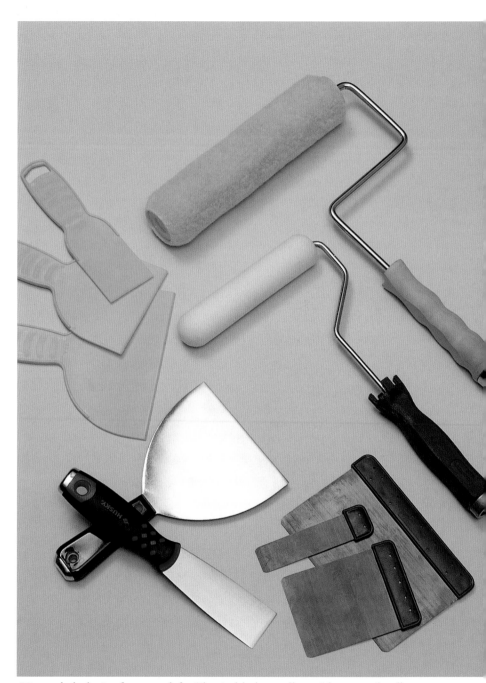

Pictured above: Sanding the sharp corners of a blade.

Pictured clockwise from top left: Plastic blades, roller with napped roller cover, foam roller, metal "spatula" blades, metal blades with handles.

ROLLERS

Paint rollers can be used to apply textured plaster. A roller cover with 3/8" nap works well. It's important to use a good quality roller cover for applying glazes; you may use a lesser quality, less expensive cover to apply plaster.

You also can use a foam roller; choose one with dense foam. They usually come in 6" or 8" widths.

Tools & Supplies for Preparing & Protecting Surfaces

Working with plaster is much easier if you take the time to properly prepare surfaces and protect the area where you will be working from spills and drips and spatters. You'll need these supplies:

Heavy duty drop cloths or tarps, to protect floors and furniture and prevent paint, glaze, and plaster spills or spackle from seeping through.

Painter's tape, to mask off moldings and other wood trim. High quality painter's tape is recommended; choose the type that can be left safely on surfaces for up to seven days.

Trisodium phosphate, for cleaning grease, grime, and fingerprints from walls. This powdered cleaning agent is sold at hardware and paint stores.

Sandpaper, for smoothing surfaces. You'll need a variety of grits – 80, 100, 200, 600.

Sanding block, for sanding flat surfaces. You can use it with any grit of sandpaper.

Tack cloth, for wiping away sanding dust. This oil-saturated cloth removes loose debris from surfaces.

Soft rags, for wiping up spills. Boxed rags can be purchased at paint store and hardware stores. You can also use **shop towels**, which are heavy duty paper towels available in rolls or boxes.

Chalk pencil, for marking. The chalk is easily rubbed off walls.

Rulers and yardsticks, for measuring. Having different lengths will accommodate small and large spaces. For determining square footage, a 25-ft. **measuring tape** is useful.

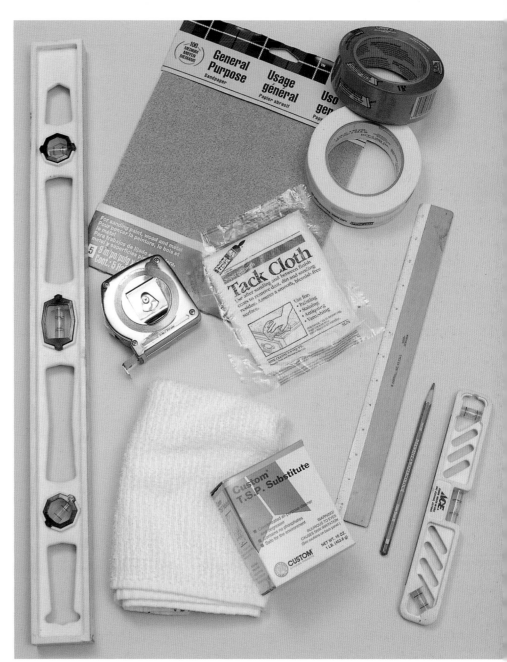

Pictured clockwise from center top: Sandpaper, painter's tape, tack cloth, ruler, chalk pencil, short level, trisodium phosphate cleaner, rags, measuring tape, long carpenter's level.

Carpenter's level, for determining horizontal and vertical lines. It may be metal, plastic, or wood; various lengths are available.

17

Tools & Supplies for Creating Decorative Effects

Stippler brushes with nylon or natural hair bristles are used to create texture on glaze or plaster. They come in various sizes and styles, including large ones that resemble a shoe polishing brush and ones with handles that resemble paint brushes and have different lengths of bristles.

Chip brushes are inexpensive flat paint brushes with china (natural) bristles that are used to apply plaster and glaze; they are especially useful when working in corners. Chip brushes come in various widths; I use ones from 1/2" to 4".

Grout tape is narrow self-adhesive tape (usually 1/4" wide) for creating grout lines for faux tiles. The tape is applied to the surface, plaster is applied over the surface, and the tape is removed, forming "grout" lines between plaster "tiles" and revealing the color of the surface on which it was applied. Find grout tape at major craft stores in the section with stenciling supplies.

Lace fabric, manufactured for making curtains and sold by the yard, is used to create the Venetian lace technique on walls. Lace made from polyester or synthetic blends works best because it stretches out of shape less readily than cotton.

Decorative plaster is an acrylic paste that is used to create decorative effects.

Crackle paste is an acrylic plaster-like paste that produces cracks in the surface of paint or plaster, allowing the background color to show through.

Pictured clockwise from top left: Crackle paste, natural sponge, lace fabric, grout tape, three chip brushes (medium, large, small), stippler brush.

Crackle Medium is of glue-like consistency. It is applied between the paint layer and the plaster layer. When plaster is applied over crackle medium, cracks are created in the plaster.

continued on page 20

Pictured clockwise from top: Metal combs, rubber comb, pre-cut stencil, acrylic paint, foam stamps. *At the center, left to right:* Stencil brush, artist's paint brushes.

Tools for Creating Decorative Effects, continued.

Natural sponges – also called sea sponges – are used for creating texture on plaster and applying glazes. They come in a variety of sizes from small to large size and are available at hardware, crafts, and paint stores.

Combs are available in rubber and metal in various widths and tooth sizes. They create lines when dragged through wet glaze or plaster.

Stamps – made of foam or rubber – can be pressed into wet plaster to create designs. Use them as spot motifs or to create borders.

Stencils can be used to create raised designs – wet plaster is applied through the stencil openings with a blade. You can buy pre-cut stencils in a huge variety of motifs or cut your own from sheets of stencil blank material. Stencils made of mylar (a transparent plastic material) are best for working with plaster.

Stencil paints are acrylic paints designed especially for stenciling. They can be used for stenciling on plaster or for coloring raised or recessed plaster effects.

Stencil brushes are round brushes with short bristles made especially for stenciling.

Artist's paint brushes, which come in a variety of types and sizes, are used for decorative painting. Synthetic bristle brushes are generally used for applying waterbase paints and glazes.

Topcoats & Other Supplies

TOPCOATS

A topcoat adds protection to a plastered wall and makes it washable. There are two types of topcoats you may use.

The first type of topcoat is thick and gel-like. It is made specifically to be applied with a metal blade. It adds sheen – satin or gloss. It may be applied clear or have mica powders or iridescent pigments added to them that impart a pearlescent finish. You can also add your own universal tints to a clear topcoat to achieve a sheer color for a particular effect. This type of topcoat is used with polished plaster.

The other type of topcoat is a waterbased urethane designed to be rolled on. It can be matte or add a sheen. This type of topcoat would not be tinted.

For best results, it's a good idea to use the topcoat the plaster manufacturer recommends. Some plaster product manufacturers make a topcoat for use with their products. If a specific product is not specified, use a waterbased urethane varnish. Topcoats are available in gallon and quart containers.

Purchase the topcoat product when you purchase your plaster. All topcoats should be waterbased.

OTHER SUPPLIES

Paint tray – the kind usually used with a paint roller – is used for holding plaster and glazes. Using a disposable liner makes cleanup quick and easy.

Water bucket, to be filled with water for cleaning tools as you work and when you're finished. A two-gallon size plastic bucket is recommended.

Pictured at right, clockwise from top right: Dead flat varnish, untinted topcoat, tinted topcoat, metal blade for applying topcoat, waterbased urethane varnish, soft rag, paint roller, paint tray.

Selecting Your Color

Choosing colors for the home can be difficult, and color can be intimidating – there are so many choices! Things can get more complicated when you apply sheer colors over one another, as you do when you glaze over plaster. Here are some tips and guidelines:

- When using untinted plaster, you only need to be concerned with the color(s) that will be applied on top. When tinting the plaster first, remember that the color of the plaster (called the substrate color) is the base color for the glazes you apply over it.

- When two colors are combined, they produce a third color that is the one your eyes see. For example, if you glaze a wall with blue and yellow, you may visualize it with blue areas and yellow areas, independent of one another. But unless you have created stripes of each color, the final result will be green.

COLOR THEORY

A color wheel is a tool used as a reference when discussing color. It is based on twelve colors that are divided into three categories:

Primary Colors – red, yellow, and blue – cannot be created from other colors. When these colors are mixed, they create the other colors on the wheel. The colors produced are the families into which all subsequent colors are organized.

Secondary Colors are mixes of two primary colors:

Blue + Yellow = Green

Red + Yellow = Orange

Red + Blue = Violet

Intermediate or tertiary colors consist of a primary color mixed with a secondary color:

Yellow + Green (B + Y) = Yellow Green

Blue + Green (B + Y) = Blue Green

Blue + Violet (B + R) = Blue Violet

Red + Violet (B + R) = Red Violet

Red + Orange (R + Y) = Red Orange

Yellow + Orange (R + Y) = Yellow Orange

Color Schemes

MONOCHROMATIC

A monochromatic color scheme consists of various values or shades of one color.

COMPLEMENTARY

Complementary color schemes are composed of colors that are opposite each on the color wheel.

TRIADIC

A triadic color scheme includes three colors that are equidistantly spaced on the color wheel.

SPLIT COMPLEMENTARY

A split complementary color scheme uses a main color split into two neighboring colors.

Color Terms

Hue is the name for pure colors.

Value refers to how light or how dark a color is on a scale of grays.

Tint refers to raising the value of a color. This can be done by adding white or by using a color above the normal hue.

Shade refers to lowering the value of a color. This can be done by adding black to the color or by using a color below the normal hue.

Intensity or **chroma** is the brightness or dullness of a color, or the purity of the hue. Full intensity is at normal value and is pure. To tone a color, use the complementary color – the color which lies opposite it on the color wheel – or an earth color such as raw umber or burnt sienna. To reduce intensity, add white for a lighter value or black for a darker value.

Opacity and **transparency**: An opaque color blocks the passage of radiant light and is difficult to see through. A transparent color is clear enough to be seen through, allowing the color underneath it to be seen. (Glazes are transparent colors.) An opaque color can be made transparent by adding a medium that dilutes the pigment. (Example: Tinting transparent glazing medium with opaque acrylic paint creates a transparent glaze.)

WARM OR COOL?

Colors are considered either warm or cool. Warm colors are hues that will cause a color to advance (seem closer). Cool colors cause a subject to spatially recede (seem farther away). Here are some examples:

Warm Colors

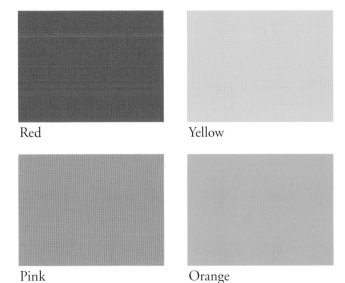

Red

Yellow

Pink

Orange

Cool Colors

Blue

Green

Gray

Earth Colors

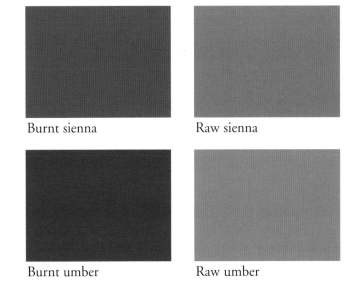

Burnt sienna

Raw sienna

Burnt umber

Raw umber

Glossary

Acrylic – A paint in which the vehicle is acrylic resin. Acrylic paints are fast drying and can be cleaned up with soap and water while wet.

Blades – Metal or plastic tools for applying plaster. The *action blade* is the blade that delivers the plaster to the surface; the *loading blade* scoops the plaster from the container and is used to load the action blade.

Breakthrough – Plaster application technique that leaves some areas of substrate (the surface beneath the plaster) visible (breaking through).

Burnish – Circular movement used to polish plaster or other surface.

Chair rail – Decorative molding applied horizontally to a wall, usually at the height of a chair's back.

Chatter – Dragging the plaster blade while rocking your hand to create irregular texture as you unload the blade.

Cross hatch – A technique of plaster application. Applying in one direction, then in an opposing direction.

Dry brushing – Dipping a brush in paint or glaze, then blotting or dabbing the brush to remove most of the paint or glaze so very little remains before touching the brush to the surface.

Eggshell finish – A low sheen finish with an appearance like the shell of an egg.

Fresco – The art of painting on fresh (wet, not dry) plaster.

Frieze – An ornamental, often sculptured band extending around a room.

Glazing Medium – A transparent coating, tinted or untinted, applied to surface. Some glazes are self-sealing, others are not.

Holidays – Painter's term for bare spots on a wall. A painter who leaves too many unpainted spots may get an unpaid "holiday" – no work, no pay – at the order of the crew chief.

Opaque – The quality of blocking the passage of light so a surface appears solid.

Satin finish – Higher gloss than low sheen (eggshell), but not as glossy as semi-gloss.

Stencil – A cutout design in a paint-resistant surface through which paint or plaster can be applied to a surface.

Stipple – A raised textured area in paint or plaster.

Stippling – A method of pouncing with a brush or sponge to create texture in paint or plaster.

Substrate – The base on which paint or plaster is applied.

Topcoat – A product that protects a decorated surface. For plaster, the topcoat is water-based. It can be gel-like or liquid.

Translucent – Clear enough to let light pass through.

Wainscot – The lower part of an interior wall, typically separated from the upper part by a decorative molding.

Waterbased – Water soluble, non-alkyd based glaze, paint, or varnish.

Preparing Your Surface

Proper surface preparation is vital for a good plaster result. Depending on the condition
and type of surface you are working on, you may not need to follow all these steps.

1. **Protect the area.** Before beginning any project, prepare the general area. Remove any clutter. Cover floors with tarps or heavy drop cloths. Also cover all furniture and counters.

2. **Sand.** Sand satin or semi-gloss surfaces with coarse (80 to 110 grit) sandpaper to give the surface "tooth" for better plaster adhesion. Plaster will not adhere to a slippery surface. You also need to sand away bumps and areas of heavy stipple.

3. **Clean.** The surface must be free of dirt, glue, chalking (white powder on the surface), and oils.
   • Be sure to remove all the wallpaper glue if you have removed wallpaper; any glue that remains can cause the plaster to crackle and/or not adhere well in those areas.
   • Washing previously painted surfaces with a trisodium phosphate solution is recommended. Follow the package instructions and let dry completely.

4. **Smooth.** Fill nicks and gouges with crack filler, spackling compound, or putty and let dry. Sand smooth. This is especially necessary when creating polished plaster or Venetian plaster. If the plaster effect will be uneven, not smooth, it is less critical that the wall be perfectly smooth when you start.

5. **Wipe.** Use a tack cloth or a damp rag to remove any dust. *Option:* Vacuum.

6. **Mask off.** Tape off the ceiling line and opposite walls at corners. (See the photo) It's a good idea to tape off molding and other woodwork as well to protect it.

7. **Organize.** Gather your tools and supplies and organize them on a folding table in one area of the room.

AS YOU WORK & WHEN YOU'RE FINISHED

To keep your tools in good condition and avoid unwanted grit in your finished plaster, **always** clean tools with warm, soapy water and rinse them thoroughly. Dry metal blades thoroughly to keep them from rusting.

Masking off in preparation for plastering.

Raised plaster leaves
created with a stencil

See page 118 for details.

Creating Polished Plaster Walls

IN THE HOME, POLISHED PLASTER IMPARTS A sophisticated design element with a sense of beauty and permanence like that of fine marble. It is typically applied with flexible blades in layers to create the illusion of a textured surface. It dries to a hard, durable finish, and can be burnished to a high sheen.

Polished plaster can be applied over previously painted surfaces and over plaster, wood, metal, and plastic. It is quick drying – many layers can be applied on the same day – and is usually sold in gallon containers, though some manufacturers do feature quart sizes.

Polished plaster can be tinted with artist's acrylic paints, universal tints, and metallic, iridescent, and pearlescent powders. When tinting plaster to a deep color, a clear base plaster is recommended because it's easier to mix a darker color in a clear base than in a white untinted plaster base. Using a clear base plaster and topcoat will allow more shimmer to be visible if you've used iridescent pigments. Clear base plasters are most readily available from online and mail order outlets.

Continued on page 32

Pictured at right: Polished plaster stripes. See page 46 for a description of this powder room.

Continued from page 30

When the plaster is fully cured and a topcoat has been applied, the plaster is washable. Topcoats are available in quart and gallon sizes.

In the instructions that follow, you'll see how to create one-color and two-color polished plaster walls. To create polished plaster, you can use either metal or plastic blades. The photo series that follows shows the steps for creating polished plaster – first with metal blades, then with plastic blades.

One-Color Polished Plaster

Supplies to Gather

PLASTER
Plaster may be labeled "Venetian plaster," "Italian plaster," or "polished plaster" and is available tinted or untinted

FLEXIBLE PLASTER BLADES
Two 4" blades are needed – one for loading and one for applying (the action blade). You can use metal or plastic for applying. You will need metal blades for burnishing. You may need to have on hand a smaller application blade for narrow spaces. *NOTE: Be sure to round off the corners of the metal blades. See the instructions in the Supplies section.*

COLORANTS
You will need colorants if you've bought untinted plaster. Follow the plaster manufacturer's recommendations regarding the type of colorant to use.

TOPCOAT
This is optional if you want to further protect your walls. You can add an iridescent topcoat for added luminescence. Some plaster manufacturers sell a topcoat designed to work with their product, but if one is not specified, you can use any waterbased urethane, satin or gloss. *See page 20 for more information on topcoats.*

TOOLS & OTHER SUPPLIES
- Paint tray
- Water bucket, for rinsing tools
- Wet towel, for draping the container of plaster to keep it moist while you work
- Dry towel, for drying your tools after rinsing
- Heavy tarp, to protect the floor and to collect fallen plaster bits
- Painter's tape, for protecting moldings and taping corners and ceiling lines
- A drill with a mixer attachment (the kind used for drywall compound), for easier, thorough mixing of plaster and colorant(s)
- Sandpaper, 600 grit (optional)

Pictured above clockwise from upper left: polished plaster, water bucket, dry towel, painter's tape, metal blades, small metal blade for tight places, sandpaper, universal tint.

One-Color Technique, continued

1
Prepare

See the "Preparing Your Surface" section. Fill the bucket with warm water for cleaning tools.

2
Tint the Plaster

If you're using a pre-tinted product, you can skip this step.

Read and follow the plaster manufacturer's recommendations regarding the type of colorant to use and the mixing technique. For this example, several universal tints were used to obtain the color desired. When you add the colorants (photo 1), it's a good idea to keep a record of the colors and amounts you use.

Mix thoroughly with a wooden stir stick (photo 2) or use a drill with a mixer attachment. The colorants should be thoroughly blended – you don't want streaks of pigment in the plaster.

Photo 2 – Stirring to blend the pigments and plaster.

3
Scoop Up Plaster

You can scoop the plaster directly from the bucket or, for easier loading, place some of the tinted plaster from the bucket on a paint tray. In photo 3, a paint tray is being used.

Scoop the plaster on the straight edge of your loading blade, keeping the product on the last 1/2" of the blade, evenly distributed across the blade edge. (see photo 3 and photo 4)

NOTE: Because this a fast-drying product, keep the open can covered with its lid or drape the open can with a wet, heavy towel to keep the plaster from drying out.

Photo 1 – Adding colorant in the form of liquid universal tints to the plaster.

4
Scrape Off Plaster on the Action Blade

With the second blade (the action blade), scrape off plaster from the loaded blade, using only the straight edge. (see photo 5) For lighter, thinner applications scrape off about 1/4" of plaster. For heavier applications, scrape off about 1/2". (see photo 6)

continued on next page

Photo 3 – Scooping plaster from the paint tray with the loading blade.

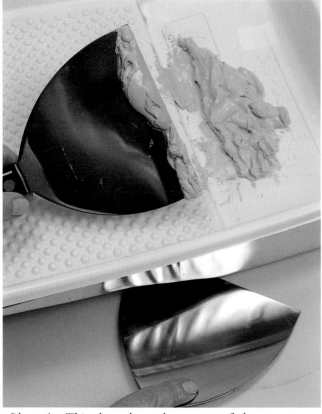

Photo 4 – This photo shows the amount of plaster to scoop. Because it dries quickly, work with a small amount at a time.

Photo 5 – Scraping off plaster on the action blade.

Photo 6 – This photo shows the amount of plaster on the action blade.

One-Color Technique, continued.

5
Apply the First Layer to the Wall

Begin on one wall, then move to the opposite wall to allow product to dry. After that, move to the wall adjacent to the first.

With the loaded action blade, apply plaster to the wall as though spackling. Tilt the blade at about a 45 degree angle (photo 7) and drag the blade across the wall, pressing it firmly to the wall (photo 8) to spread the plaster in a thin layer. Cover about 60% of the wall, leaving open areas that will be covered later. (photo 9) The plaster should be smooth against the wall – you don't want to see blade marks.

Photo 8 – Dragging the loaded action blade across the wall to spread the plaster.

Photo 7 – Holding the loaded action blade at a 45 degree angle.

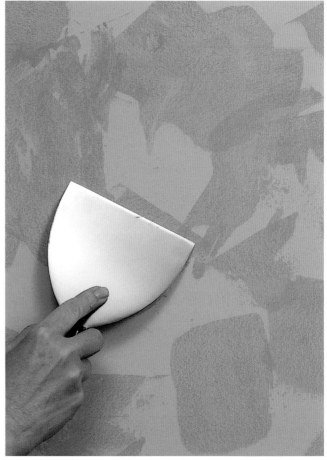

Photo 9 – About 60% of the wall area is covered, with open areas between strokes and some overlapped strokes.

6
Apply the Second Layer

Using the loaded action blade, apply more plaster using the same motion to cover the remaining 40% of the wall, overlapping the previous layer slightly (photo 10). Do not leave any of the wall uncovered. Let the plaster dry according to the product manufacturer's instructions.

When working at a corner or an edge (of a door or window, for example), hold the loaded blade parallel with the corner or the edge (photo 11) and pull out, spreading the plaster (photo 12). Use the same technique where the ceiling meets the wall, making sure you leave a smooth edge of plaster at the ceiling line. Be careful to avoid leaving obvious repetitious patterns along the edges.

As you work, little dried bits of plaster may get in the plaster from your blade. Remove the dried bits quickly and re-smooth the area with your blade. TIP: If you continue having dried bits in your work, clean your tools (see the section on Cleaning Up) and start with fresh product.

continued on next page

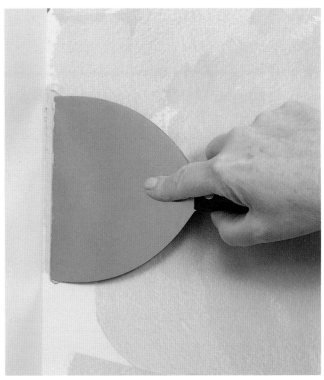

Photo 11 – Applying plaster in a corner.

Photo 10 – Covering the remaining areas of the wall.

Photo 12 – Pulling the blade out from a corner.

7
Polish the Plaster

Traditionally, the dry plaster is polished (burnished) with the metal blade. Make sure it is smooth, clean, and dry. Using both hands to manipulate the blade (photo 13), rub with a circular motion until you have burnished the entire surface. This requires some physical exertion, but the final effect is well worth it.

Option: To achieve a higher sheen, sand the plaster with a 600-grit sandpaper until smooth. (photo 14) The more you sand, the lighter in color the plaster will become.

8
Apply Topcoat

Topcoating is optional, but because polishing alone does not repel stains or protect the plaster from the oils in one's hands, it's a good idea to apply a topcoat.

Let the plaster dry according to the manufacturer's instructions (usually 24 hours) before applying.

Apply the gel-like topcoat with a blade, following the same procedure used for applying the plaster, but apply the topcoat in one step with full coverage – scoop up some of the topcoat on the loading blade, scrape off on the action blade (photo 15), and apply to the wall (photo 16).

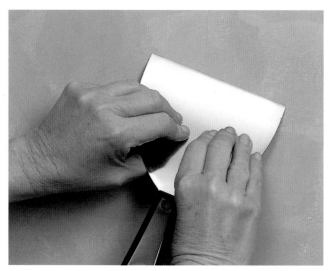

Photo 13 – Burnishing with a blade.

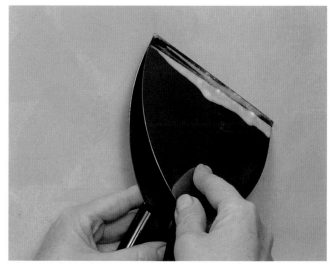

Photo 15 – Scraping off the topcoat from the loading blade to the action blade.

Photo 14 – Polishing with sandpaper.

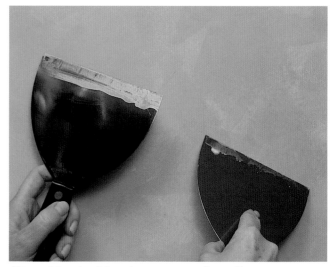

Photo 16 – Applying the topcoat to the wall.

9
Clean Up

Clean all tools in warm, soapy water. Rinse thoroughly. Dry metal blades to prevent rusting.

USING PLASTIC BLADES

You can also apply polished plaster with plastic blades. The steps are the same – these photos illustrate Steps 3 through 5 of the process. However, burnishing must be done with metal blades.

The plastic blade with the correct amount of plaster.

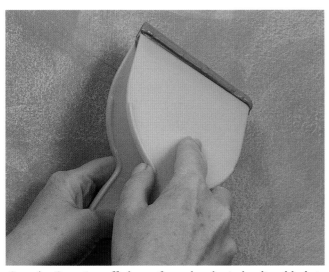

Step 3 – A plastic loading blade loaded with plaster.

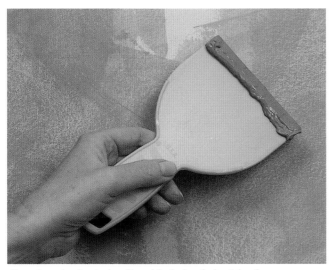

Step 4 – Scraping off plaster from the plastic loading blade to the plastic action blade.

Step 5 – Applying plaster to the wall with a plastic blade.

Polished Plaster Study

Polished plaster in two colors creates subtle texture on the walls of this study. After the first color was dry, additional plaster was applied along the edge of a torn piece of paper to create the illusion of split stone in three randomly spaced areas. A photo series showing the steps for creating two-color polished plaster appears on the pages that follow.

YOU WILL NEED:
Plaster for polished plaster, tinted with universal tints to two colors

First Color:
To 1 gallon of plaster, add:
3 tsp. raw umber
2 tsp. raw sienna
1 tsp. pthalo green
1/2 tsp. black

Second Color:
To 1 gallon of plaster, add:
3 tsp. raw umber
2 tsp. raw sienna
1/2 tsp. pthalo green
1/2 tsp. black

PROCEDURE:
1. Apply first color with metal blades – 60% first layer, 40% remaining layer.
2. Tear a piece of kraft paper to create an irregular edge. Tape to wall and apply first plaster color along edge of paper. Remove paper. Let dry.
3. Apply second color with metal blades – 60% first layer, 40% remaining layer.
4. Burnish with a metal blade.

Two-Color Polished Plaster

Two-color polished plaster uses plaster tinted to a lighter color for the second application.
The steps are the same as those for the one-color polished plaster technique.

1
Prepare

See the "Preparing Your Surface" section. Fill the bucket with warm water for cleaning tools.

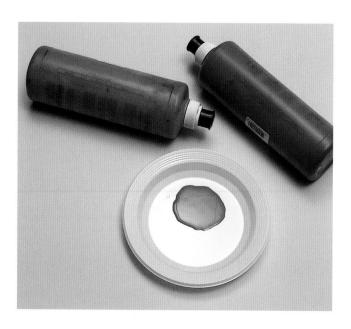

2
Tint the Plaster

Read and follow the plaster manufacturer's recommendations regarding the type of colorants to use and the mixing technique. For this example, several universal tints were used to obtain the desired colors. When you add the colorants, it's a good idea to keep a record of the colors and amounts you use. Mix a lighter tint for the second plaster color.

Mix each color of plaster thoroughly with a wooden stir stick or use a drill with a mixer attachment. The colorants should be thoroughly blended.

3
Apply the First Layer

Begin on one wall, then move to the opposite wall to allow product to dry. After that, move to the wall adjacent to the first.

With the loaded action blade, apply plaster to the wall as though spackling. Tilt the blade at about a 45 degree angle and drag the blade across the wall, pressing it firmly to the wall to spread the plaster in a thin layer. Cover about 60% of the wall, leaving open areas that will be covered later with the second color. The plaster should be smooth against the wall – you don't want to see blade marks.

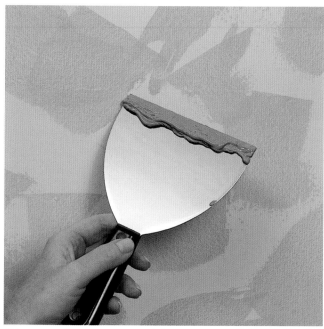

Photo 1 – Scoop up some of the second plaster color on your loading blade.

Photo 2 – Scrape off the plaster on the action blade.

Photo 3 – Position the action blade on the wall.

4
Apply the Second Layer

Photos 1 through 5 show how to apply the second layer, using the second plaster color.

5
Polish the Plaster

Polish (burnish) the dry plaster with the metal blade. Use both hands to manipulate the blade, rubbing with a circular motion until you have burnished the entire surface.

Option: To achieve a higher sheen, sand the plaster with a 600-grit sandpaper until smooth.

6
Apply Topcoat

Topcoating is optional, but recommended.

Let the plaster dry according to the manufacturer's instructions (usually 24 hours) before applying.

Apply the gel-like topcoat with a blade, following the same procedure used for applying the plaster, but apply the topcoat in one step with full coverage – scoop up some of the topcoat on the loading blade, scrape off on the action blade, and apply to the wall.

Photo 4 – Drag the blade against the wall to apply a thin layer of plaster. Let dry.

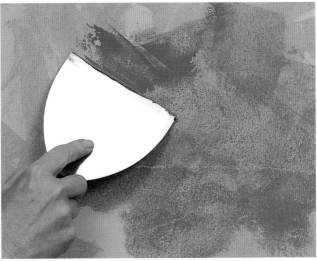

Photo 5 – Repeat to fill in the remaining 40% of the wall, overlapping the previous layer slightly.

Polished Plaster Dining Room

The polished plaster walls of this dining room were created with three colors – two plaster colors and an iridescent topcoat, which adds durability and additional sheen. Though the colors used were purchased already tinted, I've included the formulas for mixing below.

YOU WILL NEED:
Clear polished plaster base
Clear gel-type topcoat

First Color:
Black
To 1 gallon of clear plaster, add:
1/2 cup lamp black

Second Color:
Iridescent Russet
To 1 gallon of clear plaster base, add:
2 tsp. naphthol red
2 tsp. magenta
1/2 cup russet mica powder

Third Color:
Iridescent Topcoat
To 1 qt. clear topcoat, add:
1/2 cup gold mica powder

PROCEDURE:
1. Apply first color with metal blades – 60% first layer, 40% remaining layer.
2. Apply second color with metal blades – 60% first layer, 40% remaining layer.
3. Burnish with a metal blade.
4. Apply third color topcoat to wall, covering fully, with metal blade.

Polished Plaster Stripes
Powder Room

The polished plaster technique was used to create the subtle stripes on these powder room walls. Two colors were used to create each stripe – four colors in all.

YOU WILL NEED:

Plaster base for polished plaster technique
Clear topcoat
Colorants – Raw sienna, burnt sienna, raw umber, burnt umber, white
Painter's tape

First Color:

Stripe 1
To 1 gallon of plaster base, add:
3 tsp. raw sienna
1 tsp. burnt sienna
1 tsp. raw umber
1 tsp. burnt umber

Stripe 2
To 1 gallon of plaster base, add:
5 tsp. burnt sienna
2 tsp. raw sienna
2 tsp. raw umber
2 tsp. burnt umber

Second Color

Stripe 1
To 1 gallon of the first color for stripe 1, add:
1/4 cup white tint

Stripe 2
To 1 gallon of the first color for stripe 2, add:
1/4 white tint

PROCEDURE:

1. Measure placement of stripes and mark with chalk on the wall, using a level. Use painter's tape to mask off stripe 1.
2. Apply the first color to stripe 1 with metal blades for 60% coverage.
3. Apply second color to stripe 1 with metal blades to complete coverage (40%). Let dry completely.
4. Use painter's tape to mask off stripe 2.
5. Apply first color to stripe 2 with metal blades for 60% coverage.
6. Apply second color to stripe 2 with metal blades to complete coverage (40%). Let dry.
7. Burnish finished wall with metal blade.
8. Apply a clear topcoat with metal blades.

Peach Polished Plaster

YOU WILL NEED:

1 gallon pre-tinted peach polished
 plaster *or* untinted polished
 plaster base
Colorants (if not using pre-tinted
 plaster) – Raw umber, burnt
 sienna, burnt umber

Peach Mix
*To one gallon untinted plaster base,
add:*
2 tbsp. burnt sienna
2 tbsp. burnt umber

PROCEDURE:

1. Apply peach plaster in two layers –
 60% coverage in crosshatch manner, then fill in remaining 40%.
2. Burnish then sand.

Terra Cotta
Polished Plaster

YOU WILL NEED:

1 gallon pre-tinted terra cotta
polished plaster *or* untinted
polished plaster base
Colorants (if not using pre-tinted
plaster) – Raw umber, burnt
sienna, burnt umber

Terra Cotta Mix
*To one gallon untinted plaster base,
add:*
1/4 cup raw umber
3 tbsp. burnt sienna
3 tbsp. burnt umber

PROCEDURE:

1. Apply terra cotta plaster in two layers – 60% coverage in crosshatch
manner, then fill in remaining
40%.
2. Burnish and sand.

Red Sparkle
Polished Plaster

YOU WILL NEED:

1 gallon clear polished plaster base
Colorants – Red, gold mica powder

Red Sparkle Mix
To one gallon clear plaster base, add:
1 cup red
1/2 cup gold mica powder
Note: If clear base is not used, the
color will be less intense.

PROCEDURE:

1. Apply red sparkle mix in two
   layers with metal blade in crosshatch pattern – 60% first layer,
   40% second layer.
2. Burnish and sand.

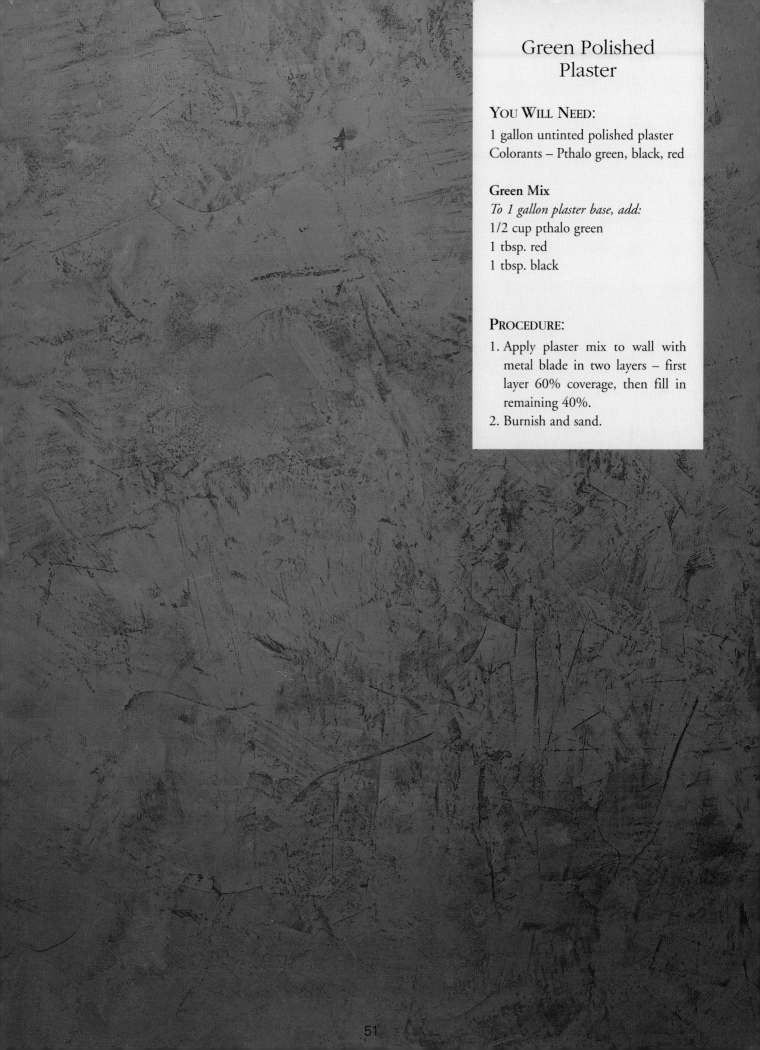

Green Polished Plaster

YOU WILL NEED:

1 gallon untinted polished plaster
Colorants – Pthalo green, black, red

Green Mix
To 1 gallon plaster base, add:
1/2 cup pthalo green
1 tbsp. red
1 tbsp. black

PROCEDURE:

1. Apply plaster mix to wall with metal blade in two layers – first layer 60% coverage, then fill in remaining 40%.
2. Burnish and sand.

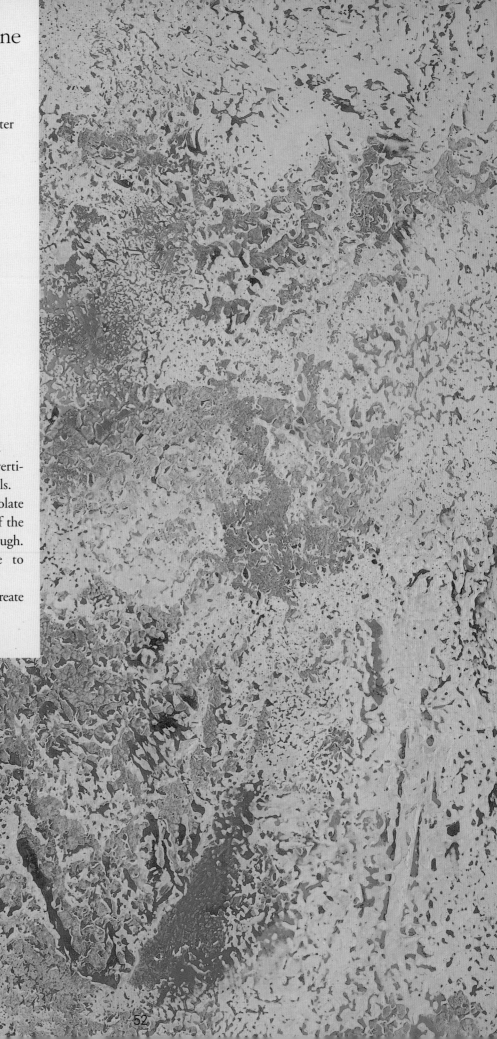

Cream & Brown Stone Polished Plaster

YOU WILL NEED:

2 gallons untinted polished plaster base

Colorants – Raw umber, burnt sienna, yellow

Off white wall paint

Chocolate Brown Mix

To 1 gallon plaster base, add:
1/4 cup raw umber
1/4 cup burnt sienna

Cream Mix

1/4 cup burnt umber
1 tbsp. yellow

PROCEDURE:

1. Paint walls off white. Let dry.
2. Apply chocolate brown mix vertically on 90% coverage of walls.
3. Apply cream mix over chocolate brown mix, allowing some of the chocolate brown to break through.
4. Burnish with metal blade to slightly polish.
5. Add cream mix randomly to create some raised areas.
6. Burnish.

Crackled Polished Plaster

YOU WILL NEED:

2 gallons polished plaster base,
  untinted
Crackle medium
Colorants – Raw sienna, burnt
  sienna, green oxide, violet

Ochre Mix
*To one gallon polished plaster base,
add:*
1/3 cup raw sienna
3 tbsp. burnt sienna

Olive Green Mix
To 3/5 gallon polished plaster base, add:
1/4 cup green oxide
1 tbsp. violet

Sienna Mix
To 2/5 gallon polished plaster base, add:
1/3 cup burnt sienna
1 tbsp. raw sienna

PROCEDURE:

1. Apply crackle medium to wall in random areas. (This allows plaster to crack in some areas.)
2. Apply ochre mix in two layers, using cross hatch strokes, 60% first layer; 40% second layer.
3. Apply olive green mix to 60% of surface.
4. Apply sienna mix to remaining 40% of surface.
5. Apply ochre mix randomly to soften olive green and sienna layers.
6. Burnish with a metal blade.
7. Sand to smooth it further.

Lavender
Polished Plaster

YOU WILL NEED:

1 gallon polished plaster base,
  untinted
1 gallon green tinted polished
  plaster base
1 quart ultra blue violet topcoat
Colorants – Violet, pthalo blue

Light Lavender Mix

*To one gallon untinted plaster base,
add:*
1/4 cup violet
1 tbsp. pthalo blue

PROCEDURE:

1. Skim walls with light lavender
   mix, covering completely. Let dry.
2. Apply green polished plaster base
   in two layers, first layer 60%
   coverage, second layer remaining
   40%.
3. Use a metal blade to apply the
   blue violet tinted topcoat to
   entire surface.

Black
with Gold Topcoat
Polished Plaster

YOU WILL NEED:

1 gallon clear polished plaster base
1 quart clear topcoat
Colorants – Black, gold mica
powder

Black Mix

To one gallon clear base plaster, add:
1/2 cup black tint

Topcoat Mix

To one quart clear topcoat, add:
1/2 cup gold mica powder

PROCEDURE:

1. Paint walls with dark charcoal
   paint.
2. Apply black plaster base vertically.
3. Apply tinted iridescent topcoat
   with a metal blade, allowing base
   to break through.

Terra Cotta & Blue Polished Plaster

YOU WILL NEED:

2 gallons plaster for polished
   plaster, untinted
Clear topcoat
Colorants – Raw umber, burnt
   sienna, burnt umber, raw sienna,
   pthalo blue, green oxide

Terra Cotta Plaster Mix
To one gallon untinted plaster, add:
1 tbsp. raw umber
1/4 cup burnt sienna
2 tbsp. burnt umber
2 tbsp. raw sienna

Blue Plaster Mix
To one gallon untinted plaster, add:
1/4 cup pthalo blue
1/4 cup green oxide

PROCEDURE:

1. Apply terra cotta plaster mix in
   two layers, 60% first layer,
   remaining 40% second layer.
2. Apply blue plaster mix on top of
   terra cotta base, allowing terra
   cotta base to break through.
3. Allow to dry.
4. Burnish with metal blade.
5. Apply a clear top coat.

Terra Cotta and Gold Polished Plaster

YOU WILL NEED:

Plaster for polished plaster, untinted
Clear topcoat
Colorants – Terra cotta, raw umber, burnt sienna, burnt umber, raw sienna, gold mica powder

Plaster Mix
To one gallon untinted plaster, add:
2 tbsp. terra cotta
1/4 cup raw umber
2 tbsp. burnt sienna
2 tbsp. burnt umber
2 tbsp. raw sienna

Topcoat Mix
To one quart of clear topcoat, add:
1/2 cup gold mica powder

PROCEDURE:

1. Apply terra cotta plaster mix in two layers, 60% first layer, remaining 40% second layer.
2. Use a metal blade to apply iridescent gold topcoat, allowing base to break through.

Creating
Textured Plaster Walls

TEXTURED PLASTER CAN BE SMOOTH or coarse to the touch. It's created with a quick-drying acrylic plaster product that may be labeled "smooth or coarse plaster" or "stone." The terms "sculptured stone" or "faux stone" are also used in reference to textured plaster.

The textured plaster product is usually heavier bodied than the polished plaster product, and coarse plaster may contain granules of sand or glass that make it gritty to the touch. The material can be applied over previously painted surfaces, and the beauty of textured plaster is that it hides most imperfections in walls so, unlike polished plaster which requires a smooth substrate, perfectly smooth walls aren't necessary.

A variety of effects can be achieved by manipulating the plaster medium on the surface with tools. It can be tinted with artist's acrylic paints, universal tints, or applied untinted. Glazing the plaster after it dries gives textured plaster much more dimension, and glaze can be applied to both tinted and untinted plaster.

Textured plaster can be glazed with waterbased glazes, and urethanes, and with metallic, iridescent, and pearlescent glazes. A contrasting color glaze on tinted plaster enhances the texture. Textured plaster and sculptured stone are not burnished or polished.

Textured plaster can mimic simple, traditional stucco or be used to create faux tile and embossed patterns. It also can be used to decorate furniture and accessories.

In this section, you'll see examples and instructions for these techniques: Crosshatch plaster, breakthrough plaster, combed plaster, stippled plaster, embossed (stamped) plaster, raised designs in plaster, Venetian lace, and faux tiles. They can be rendered in smooth or coarse; all can be applied tinted or untinted and glazed afterward.

Pictured at right: Elegant Foyer closeup – see pages 68 and 69 for description.

Crosshatch Plaster

This technique provides overall coverage and dimension to wall surfaces. It is created
by applying two overlapped layers of plaster and leaving some raised edges for texture.
The plaster may be applied tinted or untinted.

Glazing adds wonderful transparent color to the plaster. I prefer to use waterbased glazing medium tinted with transparent color (this allows the plaster texture to be more visible); tinting with acrylic paint gives a less-transparent effect. You can select one color glaze or several different colors to enhance the beauty of the plaster. Textured plaster walls also can be rolled with paint for a more opaque look. Be adventurous! With textured plaster, you can create your own piece of Tuscany in your kitchen, foyer, or bath!

Supplies to Gather

PLASTER
You will need textured plaster base, tinted or untinted

FLEXIBLE PLASTER BLADES
Two 4" blades are needed, one for loading and one for applying (the action blade). You can use metal or plastic. You may need a smaller application blade for narrow spaces, metal or plastic NOTE: Be sure to round off the corners of the metal blades. See the instructions in the Supplies section.

COLORANTS
If you've bought untinted plaster, follow the plaster manufacturer's recommendations regarding the type of colorant to use. You'll need universal tint(s) or acrylic paint(s) for tinting glazing medium.

GLAZING MEDIUM
You will mix color with this to create a glaze that is applied to the dried plaster surface.

FINISH
Option: Matte finish waterbase urethane varnish or sealer (If your glaze does not provide a sealed finish, a protective topcoat is recommended. A matte finish maintains the aged look.)

TOOLS & OTHER SUPPLIES
• Paint tray, to use as a palette for holding plaster and glazes
• Water bucket, for rinsing tools

Glazing supplies, pictured below, clockwise from top left: Paint tray with liner, cloth rag, sea sponge, tinted glaze, chip brushes for corners.

• Wet towel, for draping the container of plaster to keep it moist while you work
• Dry towel, for drying your tools after rinsing
• Heavy tarp, to protect the floor and to collect fallen plaster bits
• Painter's tape, for protecting moldings and taping corners and ceiling lines
• A drill with a mixer attachment (the kind used for drywall compound), for easier, thorough mixing of plaster and colorant(s)
• Sandpaper
• Natural sponge, for applying glaze
• Chip brush, for working in corners
• Paper towels or rags, for rubbing glaze

1
Prepare

See the "Preparing Your Surface" section. Fill the bucket with warm water for cleaning tools. Tint the glaze by placing 1 cup glazing medium in a container and slowly adding liquid colorant one drop at a time until you have reached your desired color. *Option:* If you don't need a custom color, buy a pre-tinted glaze.

2
Apply First Layer of Plaster

Begin on one wall, then move to the opposite wall to allow product to dry. After that, move to the wall adjacent to the first.

With the loaded action blade, apply plaster to the wall as though spackling. Tilt the blade at about a 45 degree angle and drag the blade across the wall, pressing it firmly to the wall to spread the plaster in a thin layer. Cover about 60% of the wall, leaving open areas that will be covered later. (photo 1)

3
Apply the Second Layer

Using the loaded action blade, apply more plaster using the same motion to cover the remaining 40% of the wall, overlapping the previous layer slightly (photo 2). Do not leave any of the wall uncovered. Let dry at least 24 hours. (Climate conditions affect drying time.)

Photo 2 – Covering the remaining areas of the wall.

Photo 1 – About 60% of the wall area is covered, with open areas between strokes and some overlapped strokes.

continued on next page

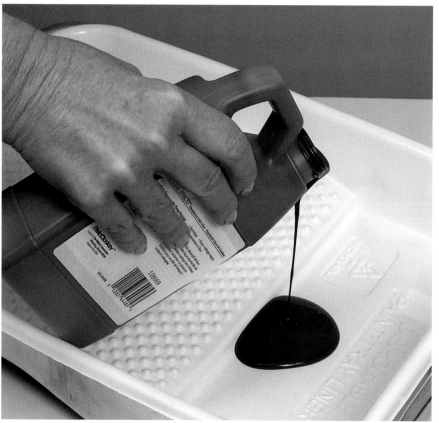

Photo 3 – Pouring tinted glaze in the well of a paint tray.

4
Glaze the Walls

Pour glaze(s) into paint tray(s). (photo 3) Dampen and wring out sponge. Dip sponge in glaze (photo 4) and dab off excess on the tray. (photo 5)

Scrub the walls in a circular motion to apply the glaze, working in an area about 2 ft. x 3 ft., leaving an irregular edge. (photo 6) When beginning a new area, start a foot away from previously glazed work and blend glaze back to the previously glazed area so the edges aren't noticeable.

In corners, use a chip brush (dipped in glaze and rubbed off on a paper towel to create a "dry" brush) to apply glaze. (photo 7) To prevent dark edges at corners, tape off adjoining corners and work on opposite

Photo 4 – Dipping the damp sponge in the glaze.

Photo 5 – Blotting the sponge on the raised surface of the tray.

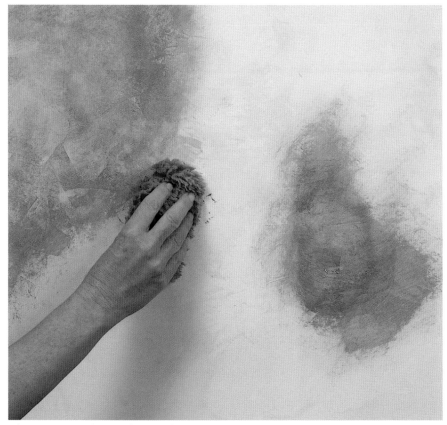

Photo 6 – Applying glaze with a sponge.

Photo 7 – Using a chip brush to apply glaze in a corner.

walls. Remove tape and let dry, then tape the opposite side of the corners and complete remaining walls.

If glaze seems too thick or too dark, add more clear glaze and a little water (if necessary). Remove excess glaze with a clean, damp sponge or damp rag.

Option: While glaze is setting up (individual drying times will vary), use a damp paper towel or damp rag to rub the glaze into the surface of the plaster to create a layered stone effect and produce more dimension.

5
Topcoat

Option: Topcoat with matte finish waterbased urethane sealer or varnish, following the manufacturer's instructions.

6
Clean Up

Clean all tools in warm, soapy water. Rinse thoroughly. Allow to dry.

Kitchen Island

TEXTURED & GLAZED

The drywall surface of a kitchen island is given a plaster finish
and glazed to give the appearance of stone.

You Will Need:

1 gallon sculptured stone smooth plaster, untinted

2 quarts glazing medium

Liquid colorants – Raw umber, burnt umber

Glaze Formulas:

Raw umber – 1/2 tsp. raw umber to 1 qt. glazing medium

Burnt umber – 1/2 tsp. burnt umber to 1 qt. glazing medium

Procedure:

1. Apply first layer of textured plaster, covering 60% of the surface.

2. Apply a second layer of plaster to cover remaining 40% of surface. Let dry.

3. After drying, brush surface with the two glaze mixtures. Blend the two colors together. Allow glazes to set up, then rub back with a soft rag. ❏

Kitchen Nook

TEXTURED PLASTER WITH RAISED WORDS

The textured and glazed walls of this breakfast nook have the look of Mediterranean aged stucco. The theme is reinforced by the words "Bon Appetit" in raised plaster applied through a stencil and glazed.

YOU WILL NEED:

1 gallon smooth sculptured stone plaster, untinted
2 cups coarse sculptured stone plaster, untinted
  (for lettering)
5 quarts glazing medium
Colorants for glazes – Green oxide, raw umber, raw
  sienna, burnt sienna, pewter mica powder
Stencil for lettering

GLAZE MIXES:

Earth green – 1 qt. glazing medium with 1/2 tsp. green
  oxide and 1/4 tsp. raw umber
Ochre – 1 qt. glazing medium with 1/4 tsp. raw sienna
  and 1/4 tsp. burnt sienna
Raw umber – 1 qt. glazing medium with 1/2 tsp. raw umber
Burnt Sienna – 1 qt. glazing medium with 1/2 tsp.
  burnt sienna
Pewter – 1 qt. glazing medium with 3 tbsp. pewter
  mica powder

continued on next page

Kitchen Nook, continued

PROCEDURE:

1. Apply smooth plaster with a roller, stipple with a sponge, and knock down the profile with a metal blade.
2. Apply earth green, ochre, raw umber, and burnt sienna glaze mixes in with a crosshatch motion. Blend by pressing with paper to remove some of the glaze and create pitting.
3. Create the split stone look by applying glaze along a torn paper edge with a sponge.
4. To create the raised letters, apply untinted coarse sculptured stone plaster through a stencil. Let dry.
5. Apply pewter and raw umber glazes to the raised letters. Add shadows with a brush around the lettering to create more depth. ❏

Elegant Foyer

Three neutral glaze colors over coarse textured plaster add understated elegance and dimension to the walls of this foyer.

YOU WILL NEED:

1 gallon sculptured stone coarse plaster, untinted

3 qts. glazing medium

Colorants for glaze – Raw sienna, burnt sienna, raw umber

GLAZE FORMULAS:

Ochre – 1 qt. glazing medium with 1/4 tsp. raw sienna and 1/4 tsp. burnt sienna

Raw umber – 1 qt. glazing medium with 1/2 tsp. raw umber

Burnt sienna – 1 qt. glazing medium with 1/2 tsp. burnt sienna

PROCEDURE:

1. Apply plaster in two layers with metal blades; first layer with 60% coverage; second layer to cover remaining 40%. Let dry.
2. Sponge and brush plaster with three glaze colors.
3. Allow glazes to set up, then rub back with a soft rag. ❏

Laundry Room

Rough-textured plaster walls were painted, then glazed for an aged look that forms
a backdrop for the polished stone of the counter. The natural tones of the straw baskets
and bamboo blind enhance the look.

YOU WILL NEED:

1 gallon sculptured stone smooth
 plaster, untinted
Cream latex wall paint
1 qts. glazing medium
Colorants for glaze – Raw umber,
 burnt sienna, burnt umber

GLAZE FORMULAS:

Terra cotta – 1 qt. glazing medium
 with 1/4 tsp. raw umber, 1/2 tsp.
 burnt sienna, 1/2 tsp. burnt
 umber
Burnt umber – 1 qt. glazing medium with 1/2 tsp. burnt umber

PROCEDURE:

1. Apply plaster with 2" blades in a
 crosshatch pattern to cover the
 whole wall with texture. Let dry.
2. Paint walls with cream latex paint.
 Let dry.
3. Sponge walls with terra cotta and
 burnt umber glazes.
4. Allow glazes to set up, then rub
 back with a dry towel. ❑

Family Room

This family room was given a stone texture and has added interest of stenciling and handpainting.

YOU WILL NEED:

1 gallon smooth textured stone plaster

Liquid colorant – Raw umber

Dry powder pigments – Brown oxide, black, orange

Beige Plaster Formula

1 gallon plaster with 6 tsp. raw umber

Pigment Formula

Mix each color in a separate container.

4 tsp. powder to 1 quart water for each color

PROCEDURE:

1. Apply beige textured plaster with crosshatch strokes, using metal blades. Apply first layer at 60% coverage; apply second layer to cover remaining 40%. Let dry.
2. Mix dry powder pigments with water in individual containers. Apply with a rag. Allow to dry slightly, then scrub with a damp towel.
3. Create limestone area around door jamb by taping off sections to create stone blocks, then applying beige plaster with blades.
4. Mix and apply three different colors of dry pigments to stone area.
5. Stencil and handpaint designs. ❏

Breakthrough Plaster

Breakthrough plaster is a decorative technique that is achieved by allowing the background surface to break through the applied plaster at random intervals. The technique creates the illusion that the wall was plastered and now, with age, the plaster has begun to break away from the wall. Glazing visually blends the areas together.

The plaster may be smooth or coarse (or a combination of the two) and can be tinted or untinted. The beauty of this effect is the random look and the it's-not-too-perfect impression. With this in mind, don't think too much! Allow your artistry to break through.

Supplies to Gather

PLASTER

Textured plaster, smooth or coarse, tinted or untinted

FLEXIBLE PLASTER BLADES

Two 4" blades, one for loading and one for applying (the action blade), metal or plastic

If needed, a smaller application blade for narrow spaces, metal or plastic

NOTE: Be sure to round off the corners of the metal blades. See the instructions in the Supplies section.

TINTED GLAZE

Raw umber and bronze glaze can be purchased pre-tinted; or select colorants to tint clear glaze

LATEX WALL PAINT

Khaki green satin latex

TOOLS & OTHER SUPPLIES

- Paint tray, for holding glazes
- Water bucket, for rinsing tools
- Wet towel, for draping the container of plaster to keep it moist while you work
- Dry towel, for drying your tools after rinsing
- Heavy tarp, to protect the floor and to collect fallen plaster bits
- Painter's tape, for protecting moldings and taping corners and ceiling lines
- Natural sponge, for applying glaze
- Chip brush, for working in corners
- Paper towels or rags, for rubbing glaze

See page 76 for procedure.

Bronze & Gold Breakthrough Plaster

Pictured at right

YOU WILL NEED:

1 gallon textured plaster, untinted
2 quarts glazing medium
Colorants – Raw umber, bronze mica powder

GLAZE FORMULAS:

Raw umber – 1 quart glazing medium with 1/2 tsp. raw umber

Bronze – 1 quart glazing medium with 1/4 tsp. raw umber and 3 tbsp. bronze mica powder

PROCEDURE:

1. Paint walls with khaki green latex satin paint. Let dry.
2. Apply untinted plaster diagonally with a metal blade, covering about 50% of the surface. Let dry.
3. Apply equal parts of raw umber and bronze glazes, using a natural sponge and a chip brush. Blend. ❑

Breakthrough Plaster, continued.

1
Prepare

- See the "Preparing Your Surface" section. Fill the bucket with warm water for cleaning tools as you work.
- Paint the walls.
- Decide how many areas of plaster you wish to apply. TIP: If you are uncertain, place tiny bits of painter's tape randomly where you might want to put plaster. Stand back and observe. This will help you visualize the placement.

2
Apply Plaster

Begin on one wall, then move to opposite wall to allow product to dry. After that, move to the wall adjacent to the first. Keep the open can covered with its lid or drape the can with a wet, heavy towel to keep the plaster from drying out.

Photo 2 – Scraping off plaster on the action blade.

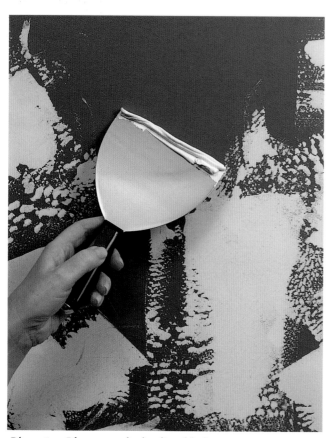

Photo 1 – Plaster on the loading blade.

Photo 3 – Holding the blade at a 45-degree angle.

Photo 4 – Applying plaster to the wall.

Photo 5 – Closeup of a "chattered" area.

Scoop the plaster from the can on the straight edge of your loading blade, keeping the product on the last 1/2" of the blade, evenly distributed across the blade edge. (photo 1) With the second blade (the action blade), scrape off plaster from the loading blade, using only the straight edge. (photo 2)

With the loaded action blade, apply plaster to the wall. Tilt the blade at a 45 degree angle (photo 3) and drag the blade across the wall, pressing firmly to spread the plaster in a thin layer. (photo 4) Cover about 60% of the wall, leaving open areas that will be covered later.

To create "chatter," where the plaster releases from the blade in a scattered application, position the blade so it is nearly parallel to the surface. Using very little pressure, allow the plaster to unload in broken patterns. (photo 5)

When working in corners, begin at the corner and pull the blade away from the edge. At the ceiling line and baseboard edge, apply the same technique. Avoid obvious repetitious patterns along the edges.

To prevent plaster buildup on tools, rinse them occasionally in the bucket of warm water. Dry metal blades thoroughly to avoid rust.

continued on next page

Breakthrough Plaster, continued.

3
Glazing

Allow the plaster to dry 24 hours. (Climate conditions may vary drying time.)

Pour glaze in paint tray. (photo 6) Dampen and wring out sponge. Dip sponge in glaze (photo 7) and dab off excess on the raised surface of the paint tray. (photo 8) Dab glaze on wall. Work in a 2-ft. x 3-ft. area, leaving an irregular edge. When beginning a new area, start a foot away from the previous glazing and blend back to avoid overlapping.

Photo 8 – Dabbing the loaded sponge on the paint tray to blot.

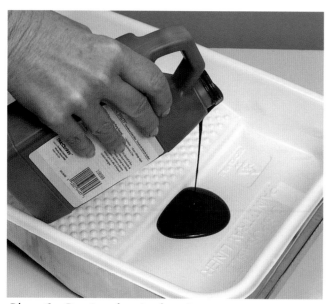

Photo 6 – Pouring glaze in the paint tray.

Photo 9 – Dabbing glaze on the wall.

Photo 7 – Dipping the sponge in the glaze.

If the glaze looks too thick or too dark, add a tiny amount of water. For a more transparent look, remove some glaze with a damp towel or clean damp sponge.

OPTION – GLAZING WITH A BRUSH

You can also use a chip brush to apply glaze. Dip the tips of the bristles in glaze. (photo 10) Pounce the brush on the raised area of the paint tray to remove some of the glaze. (photo 11) Dab the brush on the wall to apply the glaze. (photo 12) Dab and pull the brush to distribute the glaze. (photo 13)

Use the chip brush to push glaze into corners and to glaze along ceiling lines and baseboards. To prevent dark edges at corners, tape off adjoining corners and work on one side at a time. Let dry thoroughly, then tape the adjoining corner and complete the remaining walls. You can also use a chip brush to scrub thinned glaze onto the wall surface.

Photo 12 – Dabbing glaze on the wall.

Photo 10 – Dipping the brush in glaze.

Photo 13 – Pulling the brush to distribute the glaze.

4
Sealing

Option: Seal the surface with a matte finish waterbased urethane topcoat according to manufacturer's instructions.

5
Clean Up

Clean all tools in warm, soapy water. Rinse thoroughly and dry.

Photo 11 – Pounce the brush on the paint tray.

Kitchen & Dining Room

Areas of the walls were stenciled to create the brick design.
The plaster was applied, with some of it over the brick stenciled area.
This gives the appearance that the plaster is peeling away from the
bricked wall underneath.

You Will Need:

1 gallon taupe smooth sculptured stone textured plaster

1 gallon taupe coarse textured plaster

You can buy untinted plaster and add 1/4 cup raw umber colorant to each gallon.

3 quarts glazing medium

Colorants – Raw umber, burnt sienna, magenta

Stencil with brick design

Sage green wall paint

Red acrylic paint

Glaze Formulas:

Raw Umber – 1 quart glazing medium with 1/2 tsp. raw umber

Burnt Sienna – 1 quart glazing medium with 1/2 tsp. burnt sienna

Rouge – 1 quart glazing medium with 1/4 tsp. burnt sienna and 1/4 tsp. magenta

Procedure:

1. Paint walls with flat latex or oil sage green paint.

2. Stencil bricks randomly with coarse plaster, using a template.

3. Sponge the brick with thinned brick red acrylic paint.

4. Apply smooth plaster to walls with 80% coverage, allowing wall color to break through at random intervals.

5. Using a blade, apply smooth plaster over some of the stenciled brick areas to give the illusion of plaster peeling away from a brick wall underneath.

6. Glaze the entire wall with three different glaze colors. ❏

Kitchen with Breakthrough Plaster

The ochre color of the kitchen walls breaks through the textured plaster finish, creating an interesting backdrop for the natural stone chimney and dark wood trim in this kitchen.

YOU WILL NEED:

1 gallon sculptured stone coarse textured plaster base, beige *or* tint yourself with 6 tsp. raw umber to one gallon untinted plaster

Ochre wall paint

2 qts. glazing medium

Colorants for glazes – Raw sienna, burnt sienna, burnt umber

GLAZE FORMULAS:

Ochre – 1 qt. glazing medium with 1/4 tsp. raw sienna, 1/8 tsp. burnt sienna

Burnt umber – 1 qt. glazing medium with 1/2 tsp. burnt umber

PROCEDURE:

1. Paint walls with ochre paint. Let dry.
2. Apply plaster, using metal blades, in vertical and diagonal random patches, allowing areas of wall to break through. Let dry.
3. Apply ochre and burnt umber glazes. ❏

Ceiling with Breakthrough Map

Elements of breakthrough plaster give this hearth room a rustic, yet sophisticated feel. The walls were painted and glazed for an aged appearance. After wallpapering the ceiling with a map, plaster was applied to allow areas of the wallpapered map to break through in places.

Breakthrough Stenciled Walls

YOU WILL NEED:

1 gallon sculptured stone coarse textured plaster
2 quarts glazing medium
Colorants – Raw sienna, burnt sienna, burnt umber
Ochre wall paint, latex
Ivy & grape stencil
Acrylic paints for stenciling

FORMULAS:

Soft ochre plaster
To one gallon plaster, add:
1/4 cup raw sienna
1 tbsp. burnt sienna

Ochre glaze
To one quart glazing medium, add;
1/4 tsp. raw sienna
1/4 tsp. burnt sienna

Burnt umber glaze
To one quart glazing medium, add;
1/2 tsp. to quart

PROCEDURE:

1. Paint walls with ochre latex paint.
2. Stencil with acrylic paints.
3. Apply areas of soft ochre plaster randomly with metal blade to walls. Some plaster was dragged across stenciled areas.
4. Glaze walls with ochre and burnt umber glazes. ❏

Combed Plaster

Combed plaster is a creative way to add durable texture to walls. The plaster is applied with
a roller and combed with a rubber or metal comb to create lines of texture.
Vertical combing is easier on walls that are broken by a chair rail – you can comb above or
below the molding – but it may be done floor to ceiling as well. Combing is particularly
suited for children's rooms.

Supplies to Gather

PLASTER
You will need textured plaster, smooth or coarse, tinted
or untinted

RUBBER COMB
These are available in a variety of sizes and designs.

PAINT ROLLER
Choose one with a 3/8" nap. This is needed to apply the
plaster to the wall so plaster will be smooth.

GLAZE
Waterbased clear glazing medium and colorant(s) for
glaze are needed. Or you can choose pre-tinted glaze.

TOOLS & OTHER SUPPLIES
• Paint tray with disposable liner, for holding plaster
• Water bucket, for rinsing tools
• Wet towel, for draping the container of plaster to keep
  it moist while you work
• Wet cloth, for wiping comb as you work
• Dry towel, for drying your tools after rinsing
• Heavy tarp, to protect the floor and to collect fallen
  plaster bits
• Painter's tape, for protecting moldings and taping
  corners and ceiling lines
• Level *or* plumb bob and line, for determining straight
  lines
• Pencil or chalk, for marking walls
• Natural sponge, for applying glaze

The photo series that follows shows how to create a
wall with straight lines of vertical combing using
untinted plaster. Combed walls may be rubbed with one
color of glaze, leaving the vertical lines as texture, or may
be glazed in stripes (as shown at right). Determine the
width of the stripes you want and use a damp chip brush
with two or more colors of glaze to create the stripes,
dragging the brush vertically on the wall.

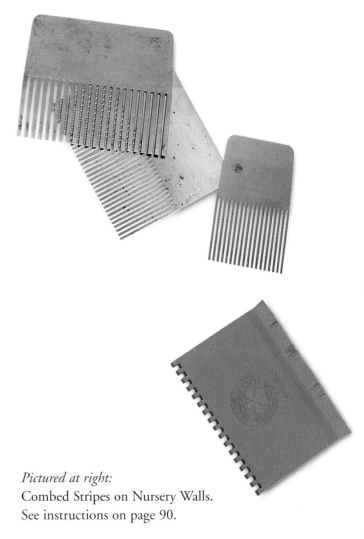

Pictured at right:
Combed Stripes on Nursery Walls.
See instructions on page 90.

Combed Plaster, continued.

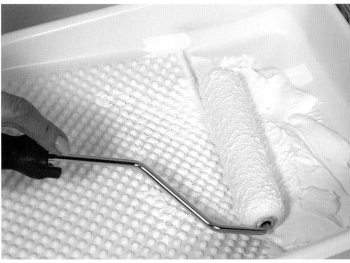

Photo 2 – Loading the roller with plaster.

1
Prepare

See the "Preparing Your Surface" section. Fill the bucket with warm water for cleaning tools.

2
Mark Walls

This is optional, but a good idea.

Measure the width of your roller plus 4" from one corner. Use a level or plumb line to mark a vertical line as a guide for rolling and combing. (photo 1)

3
Apply Plaster

Put plaster in paint tray. Load roller with plaster. (photo 2) Roll plaster on wall 1/2" to 1" from your vertical line – apply fairly thickly; you want the plaster on the wall to be about 1/4" thick. (photo 3) Drape the paint tray with a wet towel to keep the plaster from drying out.

Photo 1 – Marking a vertical line with a level and a pencil.

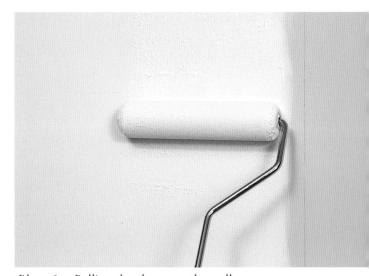

Photo 3 – Rolling the plaster on the wall.

4
Comb Plaster

Working quickly, pull a rubber comb through the plaster from top to bottom. Wipe the comb with a wet towel to remove excess plaster. Rinse the comb periodically. Use the straight line you marked as a guide to keep the combed lines straight. (photo 4)

Move along the entire wall, working in 18" strips, leaving 3" or more uncombed plaster as a wet area for applying more plaster. When you reach the end of the wall, create another vertical plumb line on next wall when you turn the corner.

Continue until all walls are finished. Clean all tools in warm, soapy water. Rinse thoroughly and allow to dry. Let plaster dry at least 24 hours before glazing.

5
Glazing

Glazing is necessary if you've used untinted plaster.

If you're not using pre-tinted glaze, add colorant to 1 cup neutral glazing medium until you reach your desired color. Pour glaze into a paint tray. Dampen and wring out sponge. Dip sponge in glaze and dab off excess on the tray. Press the sponge to the wall in a circular motion to unload glaze from sponge. Excess glaze can be removed with a clean damp sponge or damp towel. Work in a 2-ft. x 3-ft. area, leaving an irregular edge. (photo 5)

When beginning new area, start a foot away and blend glaze back to prevent dark ridges. To prevent dark edges at corners, tape off adjoining corner and work on opposite walls. After walls are dry, tape back adjoining corners and complete remaining walls.

6
Clean Up

Clean tools in warm, soapy water. Rinse thoroughly and allow to dry.

Photo 4 – Pulling rubber comb through plaster.

Photo 5 – Glazing untinted plaster.

Combed Stripes in Nursery

Blue and yellow combed stripes add texture to nursery walls. Untinted plaster was rolled, then combed, and glazed with two colors to create stripes.

YOU WILL NEED:

1 gallon smooth sculptured stone plaster, untinted
2 quarts glazing medium
Colorants for glazes – Pthalo blue, violet, yellow, white
Combs
Painter's tape

GLAZE FORMULAS:

Blue – 1 qt. glazing medium with 1/2 tsp. pthalo blue and 1 drop violet
Yellow – 1 qt. glazing medium with 1/2 tsp. yellow and 1 drop white

PROCEDURE:

1. Apply plaster with a foam roller and comb vertically. Let dry.
2. Measure and tape off 4" stripes.
3. Apply yellow glaze to alternating stripes. Let dry.
4. Tape off alternate stripes.
5. Brush with blue glaze. Let dry. ❏

Combed Copper Metallic

Freeform combing can be done in random swirls or waves.

YOU WILL NEED:

1 gallon sculptured stone smooth plaster, untinted
1 quart pre-tinted copper glaze *or*
   1 quart glazing medium with
   1/2 cup copper mica powder
Roller
Rubber combs
Chip brush

PROCEDURE:

1. Roll plaster on walls.
2. While plaster is wet, pull a rubber comb through the plaster, making swirls and waves. Let dry.
3. Scrub copper glaze over plaster, using a chip brush in a circular motion.

Stippled Plaster

A stippled plaster finish is fast and easy. Plaster is quickly rolled on to cover the surface, then patted with a natural sea sponge to create raised peaks (stipple) in the plaster. In the photo series that follows, you'll see how to create stippled texture with a sponge and a stippler brush, how to create variations by knocking down the profile of the stipple, and two ways to glaze – with tinted glaze and with dry powder pigment mixed with water.

Supplies to Gather

TEXTURED PLASTER

Textured plaster can be tinted or untinted; smooth or coarse

PAINT ROLLER

You will need a large foam roller for applying plsater to wall

FLEXIBLE PLASTER BLADES

Two 4" blades, one for loading and one for applying (the action blade), metal or plastic
NOTE: Be sure to round off the corners of the metal blades. See the instructions in the Supplies section.

STIPPLER BRUSH

Use the stippler brush for creating texture

NATURAL SPONGE

Natural sponges are excellent for creating texture and applying glaze

GLAZE

Choose waterbased glazing medium plus colorants *or* tinted glaze *or* dry powder pigments mixed with water

TOOLS & OTHER SUPPLIES

• Chip brush for working glaze into corners
• Paint tray, for holding plaster and glaze
• Water bucket, for rinsing tools
• Wet towel, for draping the container of plaster to keep it moist while you work
• Dry towel, for drying your tools after rinsing
• Heavy tarp, to protect the floor and to collect fallen plaster bits
• Painter's tape, for protecting moldings and taping corners and ceiling lines
• Wet cloth, for wiping glaze
• Plastic quart container, for mixing dry powder pigment with water (optional)

Stippled Terra Cotta

Pictured at right

YOU WILL NEED:

1 gallon sculptured stone plaster, untinted
1 qt. glazing medium
Colorants for glaze – Raw umber, burnt sienna, burnt umber

GLAZE FORMULA:

Terra Cotta Glaze
To 1 qt. glazing medium, add:
1/4 tsp. raw umber
1/2 tsp. burnt sienna
1/2 tsp. burnt umber

PROCEDURE:

1. Apply plaster to surface with a roller, then stipple randomly with a sponge. Let dry.
2. Apply a second layer of plaster vertically with a metal blade to create two raised areas. Let dry.
3. Sponge plaster with glaze for a mottled look.
4. Rub back areas where plaster is thicker with a soft rag. ❑

Stippled Plaster, continued

1
Prepare

See the "Preparing Your Surface" section. Fill the bucket with warm water for cleaning tools.

2
Apply Plaster

Work in sections, applying plaster and using tools to create stipple while the plaster is still wet.

Scoop generous amount of plaster into paint tray. Load foam roller generously. Roll on walls in sections 2- to 3-ft. wide x 4-ft. long. Plaster should be about 1/8" thick. (photo 1)

To apply plaster to edges and corners, load plaster on the action blade (see "Polished Plaster" photo series for a detailed description). Place the loaded blade at the edge and pull outward. Blend into rolled plaster until the surface is completely covered.

Photo 1 – Applying plaster with a roller.

3
Stipple Texture

With a Sponge: Dampen a natural sponge and wring out well. Pat the sponge over the raised edges left by the roller. (It will remove some of the plaster.) Continue the patting motion over the wet plaster surface, creating all-over stipple or drifts of stippled texture. (photo 2) Rinse sponge periodically and wring out well.

Photo 2 – Creating stippled texture with a sponge.

Alternative to Sponging:

With a Brush: Press the tips of the bristles of a stippler brush into the wet plaster and left to create stipple. (photo 3) Continue over the wet plaster surface, creating all-over stipple or drifts of stippled texture. Rinse brush periodically and dry off excess water with a towel.

Begin new section several feet away, applying plaster with the roller, rolling back towards the wet edge, then stipple. Continue this procedure until you finish entire wall. Begin work on opposite wall. Continue on remaining walls when adjoining walls are dry. Tape back previous work so as not to create uneven, heavy corners.

Photo 3 – Stippling with a brush.

Photo 4 – Knocking down some stippled areas with a blade.

4
"Knock Down" Plaster

This is an optional step. To create a wall with variations in the texture (some smoother areas and some stipple), simply "knock down" some areas with a blade.

To flatten or "knock down" areas of stippled plaster, pull a clean metal blade vertically in some areas, rocking your wrist slightly to create variations in plaster. Feather out the edges so as not to leave obvious blade marks by keeping a light touch at the beginning and at the end of your stroke. (photo 4)

5
Clean Up

Clean all tools in warm, soapy water. Rinse thoroughly and allow to dry. Let plaster dry at least 24 hours.

Stippled Plaster, continued

6
Glazing with Tinted Glaze

Pour glaze in a paint tray. Dampen and wring out a natural sponge. Dip sponge surface into glaze and dab off excess on the tray. Scrub the walls in a circular motion to unload the glaze from sponge. (photo 5) Excess glaze can be removed with a clean damp sponge or damp towel. Work in a 2-ft. x 3-ft. area, leaving an irregular edge.

When beginning new area, start a foot away from the previously glazed area and apply the glaze, blending back to the first glazed area. (photo 6) This prevents dark ridges of glaze.

When working into a corner, use a chip brush dipped in glaze and rubbed off on a paper towel to create a "dry brush" and push glaze into the corner. To prevent dark edges, tape off adjoining corners and work on opposite walls. After walls are dry, tape adjoining corners and complete remaining walls.

While glaze sets up, use a damp rag to scrub the glaze further into the profile of the plaster. This creates a layered stone effect and produces more dimension.

Photo 5 – Applying tinted glaze to a stippled wall with a sea sponge.

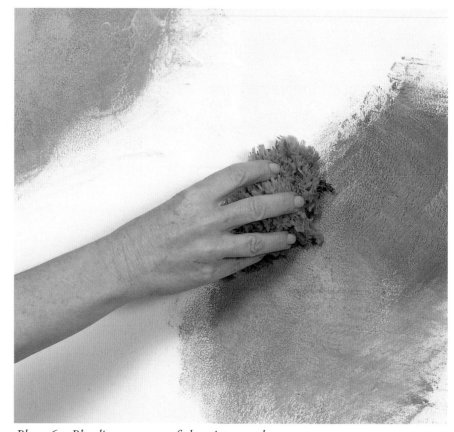

Photo 6 – Blending one area of glaze into another.

OPTION:
GLAZING WITH
DRY POWDER PIGMENT

Fill plastic container with water. Measure dry pigment and add to water. (photo 7) Stir frequently as you work to keep pigment from settling. Dip a rag in the pigment mixture. (photo 8) Rub the pigment over the wall. (photo 9)

Allow to dry slightly, then rub with a damp towel. Allow to dry 24 hours. Seal with waterbased urethane.

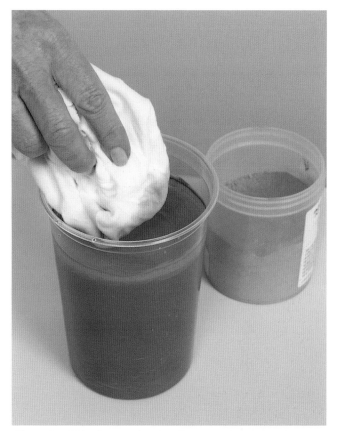

Photo 8 – Dipping rag in container.

Photo 7 – Adding dry powder pigment to water.

7
Clean Up

Clean all tools in warm, soapy water. Rinse thoroughly and allow to dry.

Photo 9 – Rubbing the pigment mixture on the wall.

Stippled Master Bathroom

Stippling and glazing add depth and interest to the walls of a master bath. A sponge and metal blades were used to create textural variations. Two glaze colors were used for a warm look. Tinted glazes were used in this example, but I have provided formulas for tinting your own.

YOU WILL NEED:

1 gallon coarse sculptured stone plaster, untinted
2 quarts glazing medium
Colorants for glazes – Burnt umber, raw umber, bronze mica powder

GLAZE FORMULAS:

Mocha – 1 qt. glazing medium with 1/2 tsp. burnt umber
Bronze – 1 qt. glazing medium with 1/4 tsp. raw umber and 3 tbsp. bronze mica powder

PROCEDURE:

1. Use a foam roller to apply plaster to walls.
2. While plaster is wet, manipulate with a sponge and metal blades. Stipple some areas with the sponge; in other areas, use a metal blade to remove some of the plaster. Let dry.
3. Glaze walls with mocha and bronze glazes, applying them with brushes.
4. When the glaze sets up, rub back some areas with dry rag. ❑

Embossed Plaster

Spot motifs and repeated designs can be embossed in plaster with foam blocks or foam stamps to create designs on surfaces. Glazing further highlights the embossed designs. You can apply the plaster with a roller or a blade.

For best results, it is important to keep stamps or blocks clean – rinse them periodically as you work to keep the impressions clear. You may want to purchase more than one stamp in your chosen design for large projects.

Supplies to Gather

PLASTER
Smooth textured plaster, untinted

FLEXIBLE PLASTER BLADES
Two 4" blades, one for loading and one for applying (the action blade), metal or plastic

If needed, a smaller application blade for narrow spaces, metal or plastic

NOTE: Be sure to round off the corners of the metal blades. See the instructions in the Supplies section.

STAMPS
Use foam stamp(s) or block(s) in the design of your choice.

GLAZE
Tinted glaze *or* glazing medium and colorants for glaze

TOOLS & OTHER SUPPLIES
• Natural sponge, for applying plaster and glaze
• Foam roller, for applying plaster
• Paint tray, for holding glaze
• Water bucket, for rinsing tools
• Wet towel, for draping the container of plaster to keep it moist while you work
• Dry towel, for drying your tools after rinsing
• Heavy tarp, to protect the floor and to collect fallen plaster bits
• Painter's tape, for protecting moldings and taping corners and ceiling lines
• Chip brush, for applying glaze
• Soft rags, for rubbing back the glazed designs

Embossed Leaves

Pictured at right

Plaster was applied with a blade and stippled in some areas, then stamped and glazed.

YOU WILL NEED:
1 gallon smooth sculptured stone plaster, untinted
1 quart deep ochre glaze
Leaves motif foam stamp

GLAZE FORMULA:
Deep Ochre Glaze Formula
1 qt. glazing medium and 1/4 tsp. raw sienna, 1/4 tsp. burnt sienna, 1/4 tsp. raw umber

PROCEDURE:
1. Apply plaster to wall with a blade, using a crosshatch motion.
2. While plaster is wet, stipple some areas with a natural sponge.
3. While plaster is wet, press a leaf motif stamp randomly. Let dry.
4. Apply deep ochre glaze with a sponge.
5. When glaze has set up, rub back some areas with a soft rag. ❏

Embossed Plaster, continued.

1
Prepare

See the "Preparing Your Surface" section. Fill the bucket with warm water for cleaning tools.

2
Apply Plaster

Work on opposite walls to allow plaster to dry.

Roll plaster on walls in 2-ft. x 4-ft. sections. Stipple all over with a sponge and knock down some areas with a blade for a varied look.

When working in corners, apply plaster with a blade, beginning at the corner and pulling the blade away from the edge. Cover the entire wall, leaving no bare spots at edges.

3
Stamp the Design

While plaster is still wet, press the stamp firmly into the plaster. (photo 1) Press the stamp evenly with your fingers and carefully lift it off the wall. (photo 2) Rinse the stamp to clean it.

Continue applying plaster and stamping until all walls are finished. Allow walls to dry for 24 hours. (Climate conditions affect drying time.)

4
Clean Up

Clean tools with warm, soapy water. Use an old toothbrush to remove plaster from recesses of stamps or blocks. Rinse all tools thoroughly and allow to dry. To keep metal blades from rusting, dry them thoroughly.

Photo 1 – Pressing the stamp on the wall.

Photo 2 – Lifting the stamp to reveal the embossed design.

5
Glazing

Pour glaze into a paint tray. Dip chip brush in glaze and rub off most of the glaze on a paper towel to create a dry brush. Pounce the glaze on the wall with the brush. (photo 3) When beginning a new area, start a foot away and blend glaze back up to the previously glazed areas so as not to create dark ridges.

Also use the chip brush to push glaze into corners. To prevent dark edges in corners, tape off adjoining corners and work on opposite walls. After walls have dried, tape back adjoining corners and complete remaining walls.

Option: You can also apply glaze with a natural sponge. See the section on "Stippled Plaster" for examples.

6
Rub

As the glaze is beginning to set up (times vary) and it is still wet, use a soft rag to rub over the design. This removes some glaze but allows recessed areas to retain glaze. (photo 4)

7
Clean Up

Clean all tools in warm soapy water. Rinse thoroughly and allow to dry.

Photo 3 – Applying glaze with a brush.

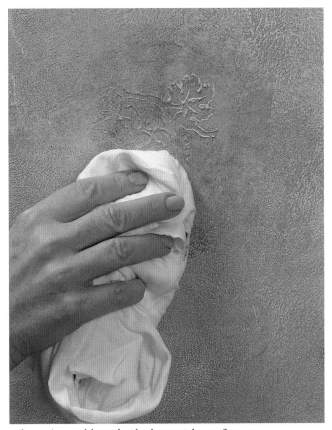

Photo 4 – Rubbing back glaze with a soft rag.

Embossed Ivy Leaves on Playhouse Walls

Even a child's playhouse can have beautifully plastered walls. A loving grandma rendered the embossed leaf design, *pictured at right*, on the walls of this playhouse at the lake! The walls were stamped, then glazed with yellow opalescent glaze. See the following pages for details.

YOU WILL NEED:

1 gallon smooth sculptured stone plaster, untinted

1 quart tinted soft yellow opalescent glaze *or* 1 quart glazing medium plus raw sienna colorant and gold mica powder

Ivy leaf stamp

GLAZE FORMULA:

Soft Yellow Glaze Formula

To 1 qt. glazing medium, add:

1/4 tsp. raw sienna

3 tbsp. gold mica powder

PROCEDURE:

1. Apply plaster with a foam roller.
2. Stipple with a sponge. In some areas, knock down the stipple with a metal blade.
3. Press an ivy leaf stamp in the wet plaster to create an all-over pattern. Let dry.
4. Apply soft yellow opalescent glaze with a sponge.
5. When glaze has set up, rub back with a soft rag. ❑

Rose-Colored Embossing

An architectural motif stamp is used to emboss the design, which is rubbed with rose colored glaze.

YOU WILL NEED:

1 gallon coarse sculptured stone plaster, untinted

1 quart glazing medium

Colorants for glaze – burnt umber, red

Medallion motif foam stamp

ROSE GLAZE FORMULA:

To 1 qt. glazing medium, add:

1/2 tsp. burnt umber

1/8 tsp. red

PROCEDURE:

1. Apply plaster to surface vertically with metal blades.

2. While plaster is wet, press stamp into plaster. Let dry.

3. Rub rose glaze on wall, using a chip brush.

4. When glaze has set up, rub back the raised areas of the stamped design with a soft rag. ❑

Embossed Pewter

An architectural motif stamp and two glaze colors create this embossed design. You can use pre-tinted glazes or mix them yourself.

YOU WILL NEED:

1 gallon coarse sculptured stone plaster, untinted
2 quarts glazing medium
Colorants – Burnt umber, pewter mica powder
Medallion motif foam stamp

GLAZE FORMULAS:

Pewter – 1 qt. glazing medium with 3 tbsp. pewter mica powder
Raw umber – 1 qt. glazing medium with 1/2 tsp. raw umber

PROCEDURE:

1. Apply plaster vertically with metal blades.
2. Press stamp in wet plaster randomly. Let dry.
3. Rub some areas with pewter glaze.
4. Apply raw umber glaze vertically with chip brushes. Blend colors.
5. When glaze has set up, rub back the embossed designs with a soft rag. ❑

Raised Designs in Plaster

Dimensional designs on walls can be created with smooth or coarse textured plaster and stencils – the plaster is applied through the openings of the stencil with a metal blade. Stencils made of more substantial material are easier to work with. You'll find a huge assortment of pre-cut designs available at crafts and paint stores, and it's easy to cut your own from stencil blank material.

When you're trying to determine placement for raised designs, I suggest placing bits of tape in areas where you're considering placing a stenciled element to allow you to visualize placement of designs. You can also measure and mark to create a definite repeat as you would see in wallpaper designs.

For a subtle monochromatic relief, paint the entire design to match the existing wall color. For more drama and to bring out dimension, glaze the raised areas and wipe off, letting glaze collect in the recesses.

Supplies to Gather

PLASTER
Textured plaster, smooth or coarse, tinted or untinted

FLEXIBLE PLASTER BLADES
Two 4" blades, one for loading and one for applying (the action blade), metal or plastic
If needed, a smaller application blade for narrow spaces, metal or plastic
NOTE: Be sure to round off the corners of the metal blades. See the instructions in the Supplies section.

STENCILS
Acanthus leaf design cut from blank stencil material

GLAZE
Choose waterbased glazing medium plus colorants *or* use tinted glaze

TOOLS & OTHER SUPPLIES
• Paint tray
• Water bucket, for rinsing tools
• Wet towel, for draping the container of plaster to keep it moist while you work
• Dry towel, for drying your tools after rinsing
• Heavy tarp, to protect the floor and to collect fallen plaster bits
• Painter's tape, for protecting moldings, taping corners and ceiling lines, and holding stencils to the wall
• Natural sponge, for applying glaze
• Chip brush, for applying glaze
• Soft rag, for wiping back glaze

Raised Designs in Plaster, continued.

1
Prepare

See the "Preparing Your Surface" section. Fill the bucket with warm water for cleaning tools. Determine the placement of the raised designs. Tape the stencil in place with painter's tape. (photo 1)

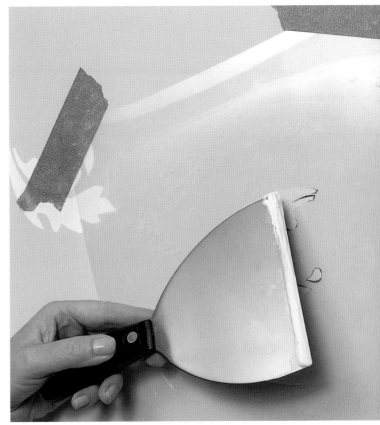

Photo 2 – The loaded action blade.

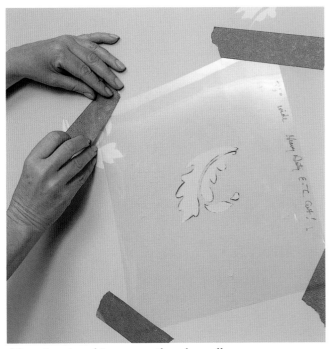

Photo 1 – Attaching a stencil to the wall.

2
Apply the Raised Design

Scoop the plaster from the bucket on your loading blade, keeping it on the last 1/2" of the blade, evenly distributed across the edge. Place a wet towel over the open can to keep the plaster from drying out.

Load the plaster on the action blade, scraping off 1/4" (for thinner applications) to 1/2" (for a thicker application). (photo 2) With your other hand, hold down the bridges of the stencil to prevent plaster from running under the edges. (photo 3)

Continued on next page

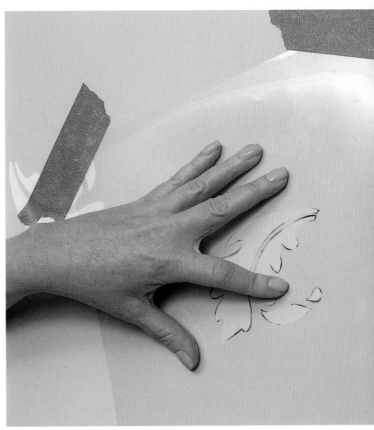

Photo 3 – Holding the bridges of the stencil.

Raised Plaster Designs, continued

With the loaded action blade, apply the plaster through the stencil. Tilt the blade at a 45-degree angle and drag it across the openings in the stencil (photo 4), beginning at the top of the design. Use a continuous motion without lifting the blade. (photo 5) It is preferable to use a heavy duty stencil when applying plaster.

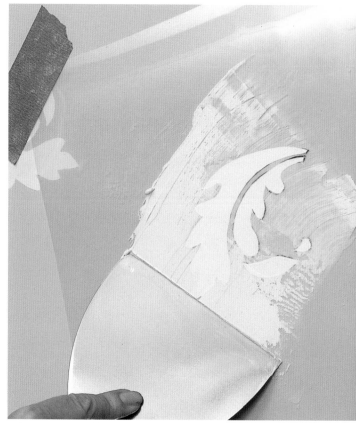

Photo 5 – Finishing the stroke.

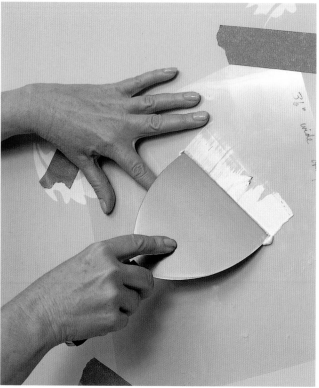

Photo 4 – Starting to apply plaster through the stencil openings.

- As you work, don't let the stencil touch previously stenciled areas.
- If you are doing a border, mark the repeats with a pencil and stencil every other one, allow the plaster to dry, and do the alternate repeats to avoid smearing.
- Clean your tools periodically in a bucket of warm water, and clean the stencils after several repeats to avoid plaster buildup on the back of stencil.

Photo 6 – Applying glaze with a sponge.

110

3
Glazing

Pour glaze into a paint tray. Dampen a natural sponge and squeeze out excess water. Load sponge from paint tray and blot on the raised area of the tray. Pounce glaze on wall over raised design and entire wall. (photo 6)

To glaze the raised areas only: use a chip brush to darken the glaze on a raised design. Dip the brush in glaze and rub off most of the glaze on a paper towel to create a dry brush. Pounce the glaze on the design. (photo 7)

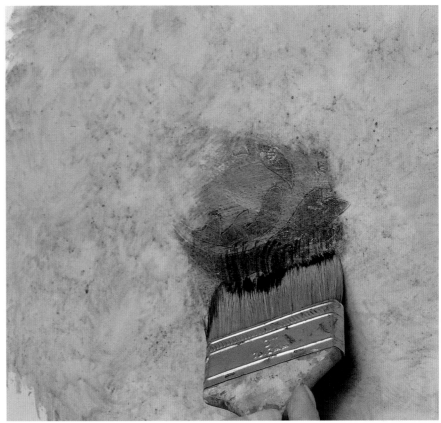

Photo 7 – Using a chip brush to apply glaze to a raised design.

4
Rub

As the glaze is beginning to set up (times vary) but is still wet, use a soft rag to rub over the design. This removes glaze from raised areas but allows recessed areas to retain glaze. (photo 8)

5
Clean Up

Clean all tools in warm soapy water. Rinse thoroughly and allow to dry.

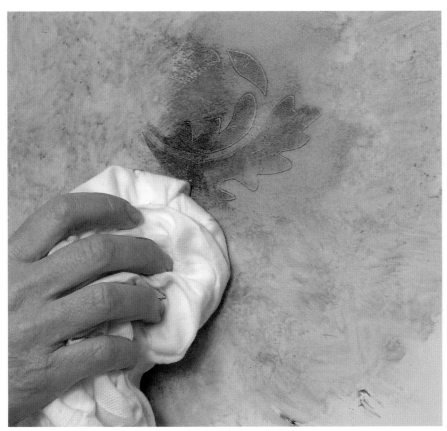

Photo 8 – Removing glaze from the raised areas with a rag.

Kitchen Soffit with Raised Plaster Design

Grape leaves enhance this kitchen soff in a soft yellow finish. The leaves were painted later with an artist brush and acrylic paints.

YOU WILL NEED:

1 gallon extra heavy coarse textured plaster, untinted

1 quart yellow glaze *or* 1 quart glazing medium with 1/2 tsp. yellow and 1/8 tsp. magenta colorants

Grape & leaf stencil

Sage green acrylic paint

Artist brushes

PROCEDURE:

1. Roll soffit with plaster, then stipple with a sponge to create peaked drifts. Let dry.

2. Glaze with yellow. Let dry.

3. Apply more untinted plaster with a metal blade through a stencil to create the raised grape leaf motif. Let dry.

4. Hand paint the raised stencil area, using artist's brushes and thinned sage green acrylic paint. ❑

Raised Frieze

YOU WILL NEED:

1 gallon extra coarse textured
  plaster, untinted
1 quart glazing medium
Colorants – Raw umber, green
  oxide
Border stencil
Cinnamon acrylic paint
Artist brushes

EARTH GREEN GLAZE:

To one quart glazing medium, add:
1/2 tsp. raw umber
1/8 tsp. green oxide

PROCEDURE:

1. Apply untinted extra coarse plaster with metal blades. Let dry.
2. Apply more plaster in some areas
   with a blade, then stipple with a
   sponge. Let dry.
3. Apply extra coarse plaster through
   the openings of a stencil. Let dry.
4. Apply earth green glaze with a
   sponge and blend. Let dry.
5. Color the raised design using an
   artist's brush with cinnamon
   acrylic paint. ❏

Raised Leaves in Bathroom

Falling leaves grace this master bath, creating a sophisticated look.
The pearlescent finish adds a bit of glamour to the look. The walls
were painted linen then a tinted plaster was applied through a stencil
to create the leaves. The walls and raised leaves were then glazed with a
pearlescent yellow glaze.

YOU WILL NEED:

1 quart smooth textured plaster, tinted with colorants

1 quart pre-tinted pearlescent yellow glaze

Colorants: Raw sienna, burnt sienna, raw umber

Linen white wall paint

Leaf motif stencil

PROCEDURE:

1. Tint 1 quart of plaster with 2 tbsp. raw sienna, 1/4 tsp. burnt sienna, and 1/2 tsp. raw umber.

2. Start with clean walls that are painted a linen white color.

3. Apply plaster with a metal blade through a leaf-design stencil to create the random raised leaf motifs. Let dry.

4. Apply glaze to entire wall with a sponge. While glaze is still wet, lightly pounce the chip brush on wall to soften the texture. ❑

Acanthus Leaf Bathroom

Random acanthus leaf motifs added to the neoclassic theme in this bathroom. The walls were
painted a rich taupe, and untinted plaster was applied through the acanthus leaf design stencil.
A warm silver glaze was applied and the raised leaves were accented with pewter glaze.

YOU WILL NEED:

1 gallon smooth sculptured stone
  plaster, untinted
2 quarts glazing medium
Mica powder pigments – Light
  gold, silver, pewter
Acanthus leaf stencil

GLAZE FORMULAS:

Warm silver – 1 quart glazing
medium with 2 tbsp. light gold
mica powder and 2 tbsp. silver
mica powder
Pewter – 1 quart glazing medium
  with 3 tbsp. pewter mica powder

PROCEDURE:

1. Apply plaster to walls with metal
   blades. Let dry.
2. Apply acanthus motifs randomly
with plaster, using a metal blade,
through openings in a stencil.
3. Glaze walls, including raised
   designs, with warm silver glaze.
   Let dry.
4. Brush raised areas with pewter
   glaze. Allow glaze to set up, then
   rub back with a soft rag. ❑

Venetian Lace

In this technique, plaster is embossed by the open weave of lace fabric for a stunning, sophisticated finish that is especially beautiful on foyer, dining room, and powder room walls. Lace fabric made from polyester or synthetic blends works best because it stretches out of shape less readily than cotton. It is available in 54", 45", and 36" widths at crafts and fabric stores. Wider fabrics are easier to use because they will cover a space with fewer seams.

Beginners may find it easier to start with an area above or below a chair rail, as it is more difficult to work with longer strips of fabric. To keep the fabric straight, it's best if two people work together to render this finish.

Supplies to Gather

PLASTER
Polished plaster, tinted

TOPCOAT
This gel-like substance can be tinted with universal tints and mica powders or untinted.

LACE FABRIC
Choose a pattern that has a bold leaf pattern motif. Close patterns do not work well.

When determining how much fabric you'll need, use the same guidelines you would for buying wallpaper – you'll need enough fabric to cover all the walls in your room, and you need to allow for extra fabric for matching repeats and keeping motifs lined up. It's not a good idea to re-use the fabric pieces as you move around the room because the fabric stretches. You can, however, reuse the fabric pieces for another room after washing and drying them, as they will have stretched uniformly.

FLEXIBLE PLASTER BLADES
Two 4" blades, one for loading and one for applying (the action blade), metal or plastic
If needed, a smaller application blade for narrow spaces, metal or plastic
NOTE: Be sure to round off the corners of the metal blades. See the instructions in the Supplies section.

PRIMER
Use oil-based primer or oil-based flat paint, for priming walls (Plaster will dry too quickly with any other base surface.)

TOOLS & OTHER SUPPLIES
- Paint tray
- Water bucket, for rinsing tools
- Wet towel, for draping the container of plaster to keep it moist while you work
- Dry towel, for drying your tools after rinsing
- Heavy tarp, to protect the floor and to collect fallen plaster bits
- Painter's tape, for protecting moldings and taping corners and ceiling lines
- Sandpaper, 280 grit and 600 grit
- Level *or* plumb line, for straight placement of fabric
- Chalk pencil, for marking walls
- Laundry basket or large bucket, to hold fabric as you remove it from the walls

Pictured at right: Venetian Lace Powder Room. See page 128 for a description.

Venetian Lace, continued

1
Prepare

See the "Preparing Your Surface" section. Apply an oil-based primer or flat paint. Allow to dry. Fill the bucket with warm water for cleaning tools.

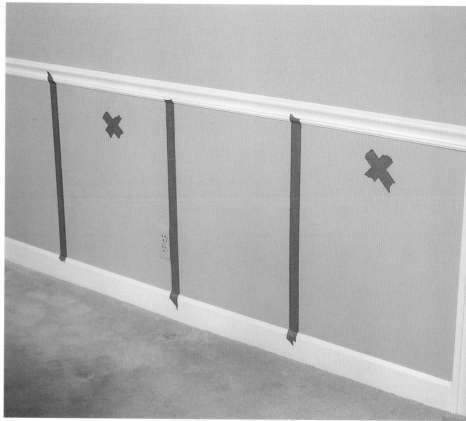

Photo 1 – Fabric repeats marked on the lower part of a wall with Xs of painter's tape.

2
Measure & Mark

Choose your least obvious corner in the room (usually it is above the door, behind you, as you enter the room) and mark your first vertical level line. Measure over the width of your fabric (minus the selvages) and mark another line. (I like to use small Xs of painter's tape.) (photo 1) Continue measuring and marking until you have completed the room, measuring into and around corners. (Example: If your fabric is 54" wide and you measured 36" into the corner, add 1/4" to each wall measurement to wrap into corner. Turn the corner and mark 17-1/2" from the corner for the next line.)

3
Cut Fabric

Cut the lace fabric into panels to fit the walls, trimming the tops and bottoms of the panels to match the design repeats, leaving an extra 2" at the top and bottom to allow for leveling.

Arrange the strips in the order they are to be hung. Number them, if you like, using small pieces of painter's tape.

You will hang alternating panels of fabric to accommodate the plaster's drying time.

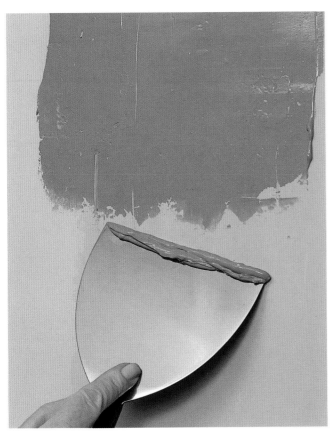

Photo 2 – A loaded action blade.

4
Apply Plaster

With your loading blade, scoop the plaster from the bucket, keeping the plaster evenly distributed on the last 1/2" of the blade. Place wet towel over the open can to keep the plaster from drying out.

Scrape off the plaster on the action blade (photo 2). With the loaded action blade, apply plaster to one marked section of the wall in long vertical or horizontal strokes, keeping the strokes as even as possible. (photo 3) Full, even coverage is necessary. The plaster should be about 1/16" thick and the wall color should not be visible. Work quickly so that the plaster does not have time to start to set up.

5
Position Lace Fabric

Holding the fabric away from wall, align the left edge of the fabric with the first level line. Allow the selvages to overlap the line and remain free – don't press them into the plaster. Lay the lace evenly in the section of wall. (photo 4)

Photo 3 – Applying plaster to the wall in long, even strokes.

Photo 4 – Positioning the lace fabric over the plastered wall.

Venetian Lace, continued

6
Run Blade Over Fabric

Run the straight edge of the blade lightly across the surface of the lace, removing the excess plaster coming through the lace and pressing the fabric into the wet basecoat. (photo 5) If there's not enough plaster to press the lace into, apply more. Avoid using so much pressure with blade that the fabric gets distorted.

Photo 5 – Running a blade over the fabric to press it into the plaster.

7
Allow to Set Up & Remove Fabric

Let the plaster set up for 5 to 10 minutes – no more than 15 – while you clean your blades. If you wait too long, the plaster will come off the wall with the lace; if you don't wait long enough or you have applied too much plaster, the lace effect will be less visible.

Lift fabric carefully from the wall. (photo 6) Place in laundry basket to wash or discard.

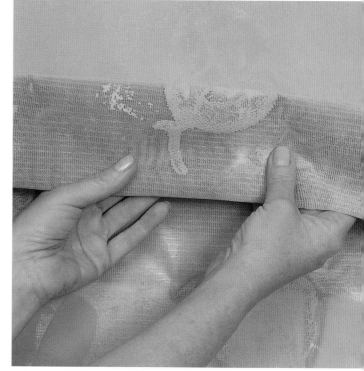

Photo 6 – Lifting the fabric from the wall.

8
Complete the Room

Proceed to next section, skipping one panel. To align the design repeats in the fabric, use a level to draw a chalk line across section you are skipping to mark where the horizontal repeat of the fabric should match up. Continue around room, applying plaster, then fabric, allowing the plaster to set up, and removing the fabric, until every other section is complete. Let dry for 24 hours.

Complete the remaining (alternating) panels.

9
Remove Excess Stipple

When the plaster is completely dry, use a blade to knock off any excess stipple. (photo 7)

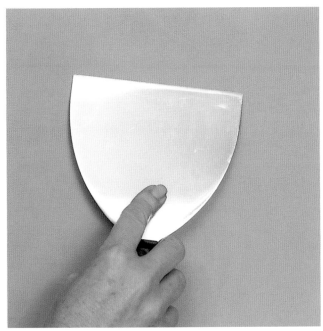

Photo 7 – Removing excess stipple from the walls with a blade.

10
Apply Topcoat

Scoop up some of the gel-like topcoat on the loading blade. Transfer some to the action blade. Using broad strokes, cover entire wall surface with a thin coat, filling in the valleys so the texture is visible. (photo 9) Let dry.

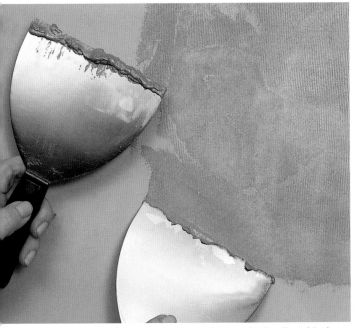

Photo 8 – Applying the topcoat. (Here, the loading blade is held in the left hand, the action blade in the right.)

11
Sand & Polish

Sand the walls, first with 280 grit sandpaper, then with 600 grit. (photo 8) Remove dust with a towel.

Use the action blade (it should be smooth, clean, and dry) to burnish the surface: Press down on the blade with the fingers of one hand, placing your other hand on top to manipulate blade. (You can see photos of burnishing in the section on "Polished Plaster.") Move the blade in a circular motion until you have burnished the entire surface.

Photo 9 – Sanding the wall.

12
Clean Up

Fabric: The lace fabric can be washed in washing machine. (Run the cycle twice to be sure all plaster residue is removed from the washer.) Polyester fabric can be tumble dried.

Tools: Clean tools with warm, soapy water and rinse thoroughly. Dry metal blades to keep them from rusting.

Pictured at left: Venetian Lace Powder Room.
Pictured above: Closeup of wall. See page 128 for a descripton of the room.

Venetian Lace Powder Room

In this elegant powder room, the plaster was tinted a soft yellow ochre color and textured with lace fabric. Gold leaf accents on the mirror and light fixtures amplify the effect of the sparkling topcoat, which was tinted with gold mica powder and applied with a blade.

YOU WILL NEED:

1 gallon polished plaster, tinted
1 quart clear gel-like topcoat
Colorants – Raw sienna, raw umber, gold mica powder
Lace fabric, enough to cover each wall - like wallpaper

FORMULAS:

Soft yellow ochre plaster
To one gallon plaster, add:
8 tsp. raw sienna
4 tsp. raw umber

Gold topcoat
To one quart clear gel-like topcoat, add:
1/2 cup gold mica powder

PROCEDURE:

1. Measure, mark, and tape off walls.
2. Apply tinted plaster to walls in sections.
3. Press fabric into wet plaster with a metal blade.
4. Remove fabric while plaster is still wet, allowing pattern of fabric to leave an impression. Let dry.
5. Knock down stipple of plaster with a blade.
6. Apply gold topcoat.
7. Sand walls with 600 grit sandpaper. ❏

Faux Tiles

You can also use plaster to create the look of ceramic tile on all kinds of surfaces. It's an easy, affordable way to create a tiled kitchen backsplash or transform the area behind the bar in your rec room.

Supplies to Gather

PLASTER
Smooth or coarse textured plaster, tinted or untinted

FLEXIBLE PLASTER BLADES
Two 4" blades, one for loading and one for applying (the action blade), metal or plastic

If needed, a smaller application blade for narrow spaces, metal or plastic

NOTE: Be sure to round off the corners of the metal blades. See the instructions in the Supplies section.

LATEX PAINT
The latex wall paint is used for "grout" background.

GROUT TAPE
1/4" wide self-adhesive tape for creating grout lines.

GLAZE
Pre-tinted glazes (In this photo series, three glaze colors were used to create a mottled look.)

TOPCOAT
Clear topcoat (Follow plaster manufacturer's recommendations.)

TOOLS & OTHER SUPPLIES
- Paint trays, for holding glazes
- Chip brushes, for applying and blending glazes (You'll need one for each glaze color, plus one for blending.)
- Water bucket, for rinsing tools
- Wet towel, for draping the container of plaster to keep it moist while you work
- Dry towel, for drying your tools after rinsing
- Heavy tarp, to protect the floor and to collect fallen plaster bits
- Painter's tape, for protecting moldings and taping corners and ceiling lines
- Chalk pencil, for marking
- Level, for marking
- Natural sea sponge, for sponging grout color
- Measuring tape, for measuring
- Foam roller, for applying topcoat

Glazed Tiles
Pictured at right

YOU WILL NEED:
1 gallon coarse sculptured stone plaster, untinted
3 quarts glazing medium
Liquid colorants for glaze – Raw sienna, burnt sienna, raw umber

GLAZE FORMULAS:
Ochre – 1 quart glazing medium with 1/4 tsp. raw sienna and 1/4 burnt sienna
Burnt sienna – 1 quart glazing medium with 1/2 tsp. burnt sienna
Raw umber – 1 quart glazing medium with 1/2 tsp. raw umber

PROCEDURE:
Walls should be pre-painted a light color.
1. Sponge grout (background) color onto walls. Let dry.
2. Measure for 6" tiles and mark with a chalk pencil.
3. Apply grout tape at centers of lines.
4. Apply untinted coarse sculptured stone textured plaster vertically with metal blades. Let dry.
5. Use chip brushes to apply three tinted glazes (ochre, burnt sienna, and raw umber). Blend glazes and scrub into plaster.
6. Allow glaze to set up. Rub back some areas with a soft rag to create more depth.
7. Remove the grout tape.
8. Use a foam roller to apply a waterbased satin urethane topcoat. ❑

Faux Tiles, continued

1
Prepare

See the "Preparing Your Surface" section. Walls should be painted a light color. Fill the bucket with warm water for cleaning tools.

Determine the size of the tiles you want and allow for grout lines between the tiles.

2
Apply "Grout" Color

Use a sea sponge to apply paint in the color you have chosen for the "grout." (photo 1) (If you don't paint or glaze the background, the existing surface color becomes your "grout" color.) Let dry.

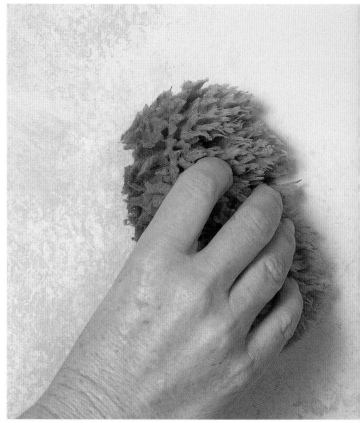

Photo 1 – Sponging the wall with the "grout" color.

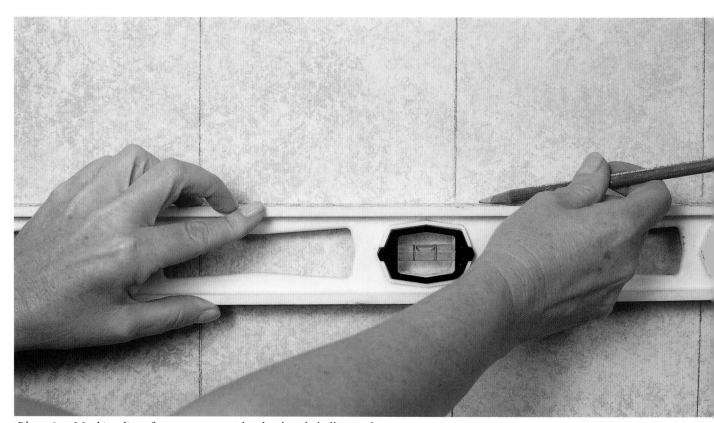

Photo 2 – Marking lines for grout tape with a level and chalk pencil.

132

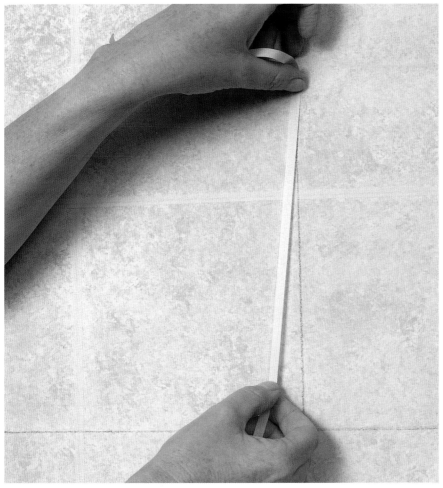

Photo 3 – Applying grout tape over the marked lines.

action blade, apply plaster to the wall surface vertically or horizontally, tilting the blade at a 45-degree angle and dragging it across the surface. (photo 4) Be careful not to stretch or disturb the grout tape with your blade.

Continue until the walls are covered. Clean your tools regularly in the bucket of warm water so dried bits of plaster do not gouge your work. When working in corners or at edges, pull the blade away from the corner or edge. At the ceiling line, apply the same technique, making sure you leave a smooth edge of plaster. Clean your tools. Allow to dry for 24 hours.

Continued on next page

3
Tape Off Tiles

Measure and mark the tile dimensions on the wall. Use a level to create horizontal and vertical lines and mark with a chalk pencil. (photo 2)

Center grout tape on the marked lines. Press tape in place. (photo 3)

4
Apply Plaster

Begin on one wall, then move to opposite wall to allow plaster to dry.

Use the loading blade to scoop plaster from the bucket. Place a wet towel over the open can to keep the plaster from drying out. Scrape off a small amount of plaster on the edge of the action blade. With the loaded

Photo 4 – Applying plaster over the grout tape.

Faux Tiles, continued from page 133

5
Glazing

Leave the grout tape in place while glazing to protect the "grout" color beneath. I prefer using chip brushes to apply the glaze to faux tiles because they scrub the glaze into the recesses of the plaster.

Pour glazes into separate paint trays. Dip a chip brush into glaze and scrub on the surface of the tile. With another brush, apply another color of glaze in an adjacent area. With a third brush, apply the third glaze color to an adjacent area. (photo 5) When working into a corner or at an edge, use the brush to push glaze.

Use another chip brush to lightly blend the three glaze colors on the wall to produce a mottled effect. (photo 6)

Photo 5 – Applying patches of three glaze colors in adjacent areas.

Photo 6 – Lightly blending the three glaze colors with a chip brush.

Photo 7 – Rubbing back the glaze with a soft rag.

6
Remove Tape

Remove the grout tape to reveal the "grout" color underneath. (photo 8)

7
Topcoat

Using a foam roller, apply a protective watebased urethane topcoat. Let dry.

8
Clean Up

Clean all tools in warm, soapy water. Rinse thoroughly and allow to dry.

After the glaze has begun to set up (test a small area if you're not sure), use a dry soft rag or paper rag to rub back some areas. This scrubs the glaze farther into the recesses of the tiles. (photo 7) Allow to dry completely.

Photo 8 – Removing the tape.

Gold Tiles in Master Bathroom

In this master bath, grout tape wasn't used, instead the plaster was manipulated with the blade to form raised edges. Metallic glazes create a rich look; 2 oz. bottles of metallic acrylic craft paint, thinned with water, could be substituted for glaze.

YOU WILL NEED:

Smooth textured plaster, untinted
2 quarts glazing medium
Mica powders – Pewter, gold

GLAZE FORMULAS:

Pewter- 1/2 cup pewter mica
 powder to quart

Gold – 1/2 cup gold mica powder
 to quart

PROCEDURE:

1. Using a level, measure walls and draw chalk lines to create 12" tiles.
2. Apply plaster with a blade vertically and horizontally. Create a raised edge on each tile by pressing the edge of the blade on the sides of the tiles after plaster is applied. Let dry.
3. Use a chip brush to apply gold and pewter glazes vertically and horizontally (in the direction the plaster was applied) to tiles. Let dry. ❑

Decorative plaster can be used to decorate all kinds of furniture and accessories. Boxes, wastebaskets, tissue holders, plaques, holiday decorations, trunks, and tables are just a few of the items awaiting your inspiration. In this section, you'll find instructions for creating and decorating a faux stone plaque, a holiday sleigh, and a round-top wooden trunk.

Faux Stone Plaque

This technique is a great alternative to expensive decorative or carved stone tiles – you can turn the area behind your stove into a decorator showpiece. Simply purchase a foam core board and trim it to fit the space you wish to decorate. Your tile can be hung alone or (if you make two) as a pair. Trim the edges of the foam core with a craft knife for the look of cut stone. Seal plaques with urethane for durability.

CAUTION: If you're hanging your plaque above a stove, be aware of how hot the area gets. Some stoves produce too much heat.

INSTALLATION: When installing the plaque on drywall, place small straight pins at corners of board and secure. Apply tiny bits of wet plaster to conceal the heads of the pins, let dry, and glaze. To install, press the pins into the drywall. When you are ready for a change, simply remove and redecorate! The plaque can also be glued to the surface.

Pictured at right: This plaque that adorns a kitchen backsplash was created with plaster, stencils, and crackle paste, then glazed for an aged look. Instructions begin on page 140.

Faux Stone Plaque, continued.

Supplies to Gather

FOAM CORE BOARD

Foam core board, cut to size desired, is used as a base for the plaster

PLASTER

Coarse textured sculptured stone plaster, untinted

FLEXIBLE PLASTER BLADES

Two 4" metal blades, one for loading and one for applying (the action blade)

If needed, a smaller metal application blade for narrow spaces

NOTE: Be sure to round off the corners of the metal blades. See the instructions in the Supplies section.

STENCIL

Pre-cut stencil with multiple overlays (bowl of fruit motif)

CRACKLE PASTE

Smooth acrylic paste that cracks when dry. Available at craft and paint stores.

GLAZE

You will need 2 quarts glazing medium

COLORANTS

Raw umber and burnt umber colorants are used for glazes.

TOPCOAT

Clear waterbased urethane, for topcoat

PRIMER

Oil or latex primer can be used for this project.

TOOLS & OTHER SUPPLIES

• Paint trays, for holding glazes
• Water bucket, for rinsing tools
• Wet towel, for draping the container of plaster to keep it moist while you work
• Dry towel, for drying your tools after rinsing
• Foam roller, for applying plaster
• Natural sponge, for creating stipple
• Craft knife, for cutting foam core and template
• Painter's tape, for holding stencil in place
• Chip brushes, for applying glazes and topcoat

Procedure

1. To create an irregular edge for the plaque, cut the edge of the foam core with a craft knife. Tear the edge by pulling the cut piece towards you, allowing some of the paper covering to tear. (This will create the illusion of split layers of stone when glazed.)
2. Prime the foam core board, front and back, with oil or latex primer. Let dry.
3. Use a foam roller to apply a generous amount of plaster to the front of foam core plaque.
4. While plaster is wet, use a damp sponge to create stipple and a blade to knock down some areas. Let dry.
5. Position stencil overlay #1 and apply crackle paste with a metal blade through the stencil. (Photo 1) Let dry. Continue this procedure of applying crackle paste for all overlays. *Note: Crackle paste was used for fruit and coarse stone plaster was used for bowl.*
6. Mix glazes:
   Raw umber – 1/8 tsp. colorant with 1 cup glazing medium
   Burnt umber – 1/8 tsp. colorant with 1 cup glazing medium
7. Apply glazes one at a time, using chip brushes and scrubbing in a circular motion to blend the two colors together. (photo 2) Be sure to scrub glazes into recessed areas of the plaster and allow the glazes to seep into crevices for a stone-like effect.
8. Rub back glazes with a soft cloth to remove some glaze, allowing glaze to remain in the recesses and cracks.
9. Topcoat with clear waterbased urethane, using a foam brush or roller. Let dry thoroughly.
10. Clean all tools with warm soapy water. Dry thoroughly.

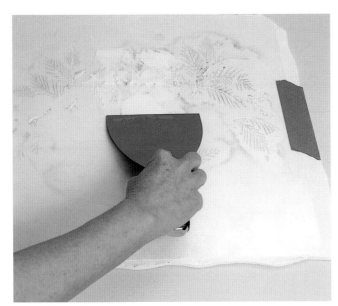

Photo 1 – Applying crackle paste through the stencil.

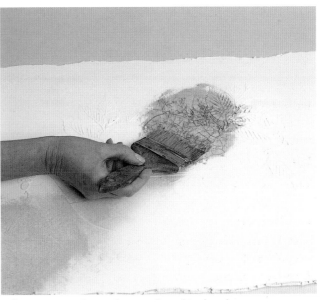

Photo 2 – Applying glaze with a chip brush.

Santa's Sleigh

You can display this sleigh on your front porch or showcase it in your foyer. It was covered with iridescent plaster and stenciled. (Patterns are provided for cutting your own stencil, or you can use any holiday-themed purchased stencil.) The iridescent mica powders mixed into the plaster give the sleigh a rich shimmer. Fill it with presents, Santa bears, kindling for your fireplace, pine cones, or anything you might fancy.

For use outdoors, use an exterior waterbased urethane topcoat. For this project, I bought pre-tinted plaster, but I've included the formulas for tinting if you want to mix your own colors. Another option would be to use untinted plaster, glaze the plaster on the sleigh, and handpaint the raised designs with glaze or paint, using an artist's brush.

These motifs and techniques can be used on any item – a holiday trunk, table, or plaque are other options you may want to try.

Santa's Sleigh, continued

Supplies to Gather

WOODEN SLEIGH

(Available from an unfinished wood products supplier.)

PLASTER

Clear polished plaster is used for basecoat of sleigh and raised designs

COLORANTS

Universal tints – Red, green, black, raw umber
Mica powder – Gold

GOLD ACRYLIC PAINT

This is used for painting edge of sleigh

FLEXIBLE PLASTER BLADES

Two 4" blades, one for loading and one for applying (the action blade), metal or plastic
If needed, a smaller application blade for narrow spaces, metal or plastic
NOTE: Be sure to round off the corners of the metal blades. See the instructions in the Supplies section.

TOOLS & OTHER SUPPLIES

- Spray primer
- Sandpaper
- Tack cloth
- 6" or 9" roller with 3/8" nap
- Chip brush
- Artist's paint brush
- Water bucket
- Wet towel
- Stencil blank material
- Fine tip marker
- Craft knife
- Paint tray
- Natural sponge
- Soft cloth rag

1
Prepare

- **Surface:** Sand wood and wipe away dust and dirt with a tack cloth. Prime with spray primer. Let dry.

- **Cut Stencils:** Trace the patterns provided on stencil blank material and cut out, using a craft knife.

- **Tint the Plaster:**
Base plaster for sleigh – To one cup plaster, add 3 drops red colorant and 1 tsp. gold mica powder
Plaster for holly and poinsettia leaves – To one cup plaster, add 3 drops green colorant and 1 drop black colorant
Plaster for poinsettia – To one cup plaster, add 3 tsp. gold mica powder and 1 drop raw umber colorant

2
Apply First Coat of Plaster

Use a roller to apply plaster to the sleigh, rolling an even, medium thick layer. (photo 1) Continue rolling, working 1-foot away from the previous application and blending back into the wet plaster. Smooth with a plaster blade. (photo 2) Continue until project is covered. Use a chip brush to apply plaster in the corners and on the edges. Smooth out plaster with a clean plaster blade, knocking down any uneven areas.

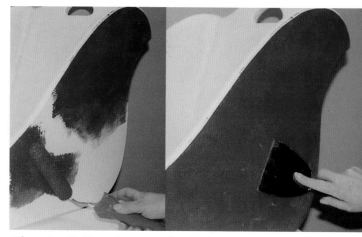

Photo 1 – Rolling plaster on the sleigh.
Photo 2 – Using a blade for blending.

3
Apply Second Coat of Plaster

Apply a second layer of plaster to sleigh with plaster blades, using a crosshatch motion to apply a thin, even layer. (photo 3) Let dry. Clean tools.

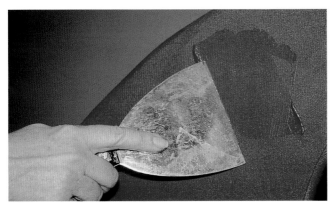

Photo 3 – Applying the second layer of plaster with a cross-hatch motion.

4
Burnish

Rub a clean plaster blade over the sleigh in a circular motion to buff and bring out the sheen of the mica powders. (photo 4)

Photo 4 – Burnishing the dried plaster with a blade.

5
Stencil

Determine placement of stenciled motifs before you start. Work every other repeat to avoid smearing previous work. See the photo series on "Raised Designs" for detailed instructions.

Position stencil and secure with painter's tape. Scoop plaster on the loading blade, then scrape off some plaster on the action blade. For light, thinner applications scrape off only about 1/4" of plaster. For heavier applications, scrape off 1/2" to allow the stencil design to be thicker or more raised.

With the loaded action blade, apply the plaster through the stencil by tilting the blade at a 45-degree angle and dragging it across the openings. (photo 5, photo 6) Repeat to complete the design, using the photo as a guide. Let dry completely.

As you work, keep plaster buildup off tools by cleaning the tools occasionally in a bucket of warm water. Clean the stencils periodically to avoid smears.

Continued on next page

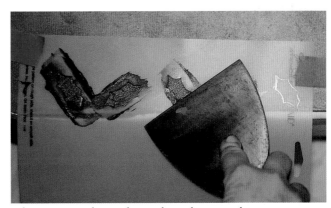

Photo 5 – Applying plaster through a stencil.

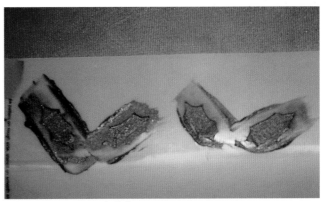

Photo 6 – A stenciled design.

Santa's Sleigh, continued

Patterns for Santa's Sleigh

6
Finishing Touches

1. Using an artist brush, apply a thin layer of gold paint to edges of sleigh.
2. Dip the tip of the brush handle into the tinted red plaster and apply dots to the center of the poinsettia

Registration for overlay #2

Poinsettia Overlay #1

Cut only solid lines

Poinsettia Overlay #2

Cut only solid lines

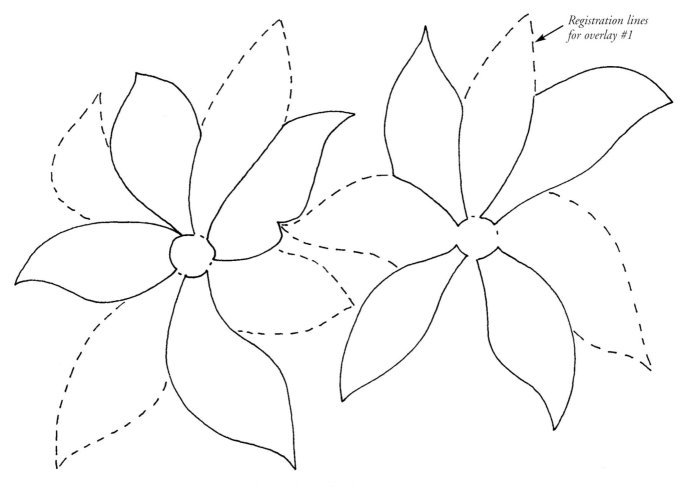

*Registration lines
for overlay #1*

*After Overlay #1 has dried, position
Overlay #2 using the dotted lines as
registration.*

Patterns for Santa's Sleigh

Poinsettia Overlay #3

Cut only solid lines

Position Overlay #3 using completed poinsettia leaves as registration.

Bottom of Design

Registration marks for other overlays

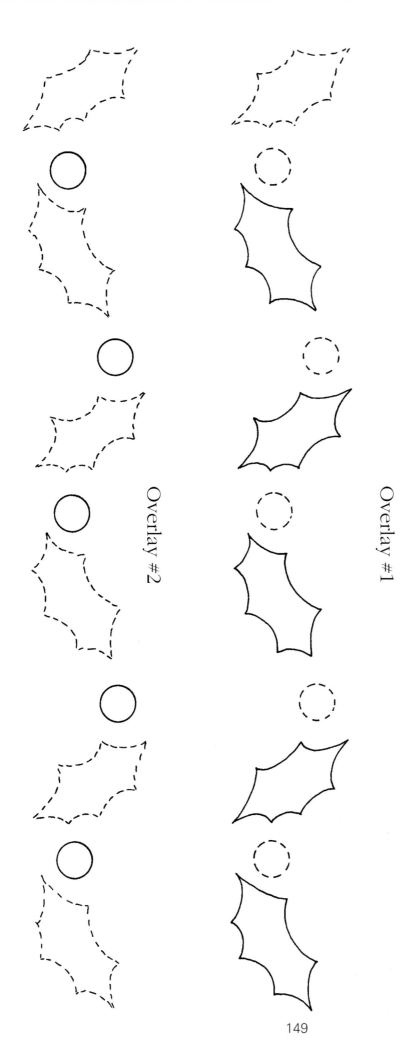

Holly Patterns 1 & 2

Cut only solid lines

Overlay #2

Overlay #1

149

Trunk

This trunk's faux woven cane and leather finish was created with plaster and glaze. It's a great accessory piece that provides functional storage – it could be used as a toy chest for Grandma's house or to hold files in your office. You could also put it in the guest room for storing bed and bath linens or use it for family treasures and photos.

The woven cane texture was created using a perforated rubber mat (the kind used as a rug pad for area rugs); the procedure is a variation on the Venetian lace technique. The plaster was tinted to a soft camel color and glazed. My instructions are for a new, unfinished wooden trunk, but if you have an old trunk you'd like to revitalize, simply sand and clean it thoroughly, prime, then proceed.

Trunk, continued.

Supplies to Gather

TRUNK
You may use a new or old (Mine is 30" wide.)

PLASTER
1 quart coarse textured, tinted plaster. Tint with raw sienna, burnt umber, raw umber, black, burnt sienna colorants

TOPCOAT
Waterbased urethane topcoat

GLAZE
Use glazing medium tinted with the same colorants as used for the plaster

PERFORATED RUBBER MAT
This was used to create the woven straw texture.

FLEXIBLE PLASTER BLADES
Two 4" blades, one for loading and one for applying (the action blade), metal or plastic
If needed, a smaller application blade for narrow spaces, metal or plastic
NOTE: Be sure to round off the corners of the metal blades. See the instructions in the Supplies section.

OTHER TOOLS & SUPPLIES
- Paint trays
- Primer, latex or oil-based
- 3/8" nap roller
- Foam roller, 2" or 3"
- Chip brushes
- Shop paper towels or soft cotton rags
- Sandpaper, medium grit
- Tack cloth
- Water bucket
- Wet towel
- Plastic bags or sheets
- Ruler *or* tape measure
- Tarp to work on
- Straight pins
- Plastic bags or plastic wrap, for creating texture
- *Optional:* Bronze glaze

1
Prepare

- **Surface:** Remove all hardware from trunk. Sand wood with medium sandpaper. Wipe thoroughly to remove sanding dust. Paint with oil or latex wood primer. Let dry thoroughly according to paint manufacturer's directions.

- **Tint the Plaster:**
For entire project, tint 1 quart of plaster with 2 tbsp. raw sienna, 1/4 tsp. burnt sienna, and 1/2 tsp. raw umber.

- **Measure & Mark:** Place lid on trunk. Tape off a center area for the woven straw. (photo 1) Cut pieces of the rubber mat to fit each area of the trunk where the woven straw effect will be used (top, front, and back).

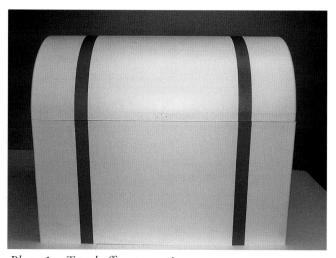

Photo 1 – Taped off center section.

2
Create Woven Cane Sections

Remove lid and set aside. Load roller with plaster and apply 1/16" to 1/8" thick to center area of trunk. (photo 2) After you have rolled the plaster, place straight pins in the holes where the hardware is fastened to keep them open.

Evenly align rubber mat material and press down into wet plaster with clean plaster blade. (photo 3) Drag blade from top to bottom until mat is evenly pressed in plaster. Repeat process horizontally.

With a clean roller cover, gently but firmly roll mat into wet plaster, being careful not to stretch mat. (photo 4) Repeat on back of trunk and on lid. Slowly peel away mat and discard. Let dry completely. Remove tape.

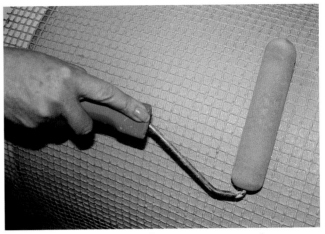

Photo 4 – Using a clean roller to remove excess plaster.

Photo 2 – Rolling plaster for the woven cane.

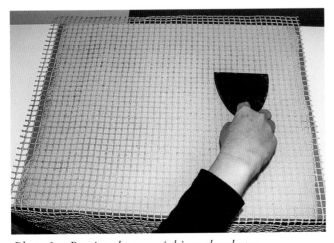

Photo 3 – Pressing the material into the plaster.

3
Create Faux Leather

Apply tape at edges of woven cane areas to protect. Load roller with plaster and roll 1/16" thick, working one area at a time, on the remainder of the trunk. Pounce plaster with a crumpled plastic bag or piece of plastic wrap to create texture. (photo 5) Stipple plaster on edges with a chip brush, being careful not to build up plaster on edges (if you do, the lid won't fit properly). Let dry thoroughly.

Continued on next page

Photo 5 – Pouncing with crumpled plastic.

Trunk, continued

4
Create Raised Bands

Tape off 2" bands on edges of woven cane area. (photo 6) Apply plaster with narrow foam roller (photo 7) and smooth with a clean plaster blade. (photo 8) While plaster is still wet, drag chip brush through it to create faux wood grain. (photo 9) Repeat on back of trunk and at bottom edge.

Measure and tape off a 1" band around the top edge of the trunk and the bottom edge of the lid. Tape off and apply plaster, smooth, and drag with chip brush.

Photo 8 – Smoothing the plaster for the bands.

Photo 6 – Taped off bands.

Photo 9 – Using a chip brush to create wood grain.

Photo 7 – Rolling plaster for the bands.

continued on page 156

5
Glaze

Knock down high areas of plaster with clean blade and remove bits of grit from the surface with a tack cloth. Mix a raw umber glaze (1/4 cup glazing medium with 2 drops of raw umber colorant). Use a chip brush to apply glaze to the entire surface. Allow the glaze to seep into the woven cane background; wipe back the face of cane with a soft rag. Let dry.

Mix a dark umber glaze (1/4 cup glazing medium with 2 drops of raw umber colorant and a speck of black colorant). Tape back cane area and wood bands and scrub the darker glaze on the leather section only. (photo 10) Soften with a rag. (photo 11) Let dry.

Use a 1" chip brush to apply the dark umber glaze to the faux wood bands. Soften with rag. Let dry. Mix black glaze (1/4 cup glazing medium with 1 drop black colorant) and repeat process. Let dry.

Apply a heavy coat of the darkest glaze to the cane areas with a chip brush. Let stand for 2 to 3 minutes. Wipe back with soft, clean cloth. (photo 12)

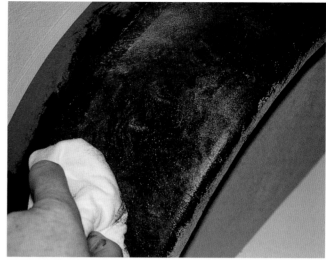

Photo 11 – Softening the glaze with a rag.

Photo 12 – Deepening the glaze on the cane areas.

Photo 10 – Apply glaze on the "leather" section.

6
Finish

Reinstall hardware.

Option: Apply bronze glaze to the bands. Wipe back on the face to leave glaze on edges of bands.

If the glaze you used is not self-sealing, seal the plaster with a urethane topcoat. Let dry.

Clean all tools with warm, soapy water. Dry thoroughly.

Metric Conversion Chart

Inches to Millimeters and Centimeters

Inches	MM	CM		Inches	MM	CM
1/8	3	.3		2	51	5.1
1/4	6	.6		3	76	7.6
3/8	10	1.0		4	102	10.2
1/2	13	1.3		5	127	12.7
5/8	16	1.6		6	152	15.2
3/4	19	1.9		7	178	17.8
7/8	22	2.2		8	203	20.3
1	25	2.5		9	229	22.9
1-1/4	32	3.2		10	254	25.4
1-1/2	38	3.8		11	279	27.9
1-3/4	44	4.4		12	305	30.5

Yards to Meters

Yards	Meters
1/8	.11
1/4	.23
3/8	.34
1/2	.46
5/8	.57
3/4	.69
7/8	.80
1	.91
2	1.83
3	2.74
4	3.66
5	4.57
6	5.49
7	6.40
8	7.32
9	8.23
10	9.14

Index

Index